AS 13

CURRENT ISSUES BIBLE STUDY SERIES

Engaging
the Culture

CHRISTIANITY TODAY
INTERNATIONAL

THOMAS NELSON
Since 1798

NASHVILLE DALLAS MEXICO CITY RIO DE JANEIRO BEIJING

Current Issues Bible Study Series: Engaging the Culture
Copyright © 2008 Christianity Today International

All rights reserved. No portion of this book may be reproduced, stored in a retrieval system, or transmitted in any form or by any means—electronic, mechanical, photocopy, recording, scanning, or other—except for brief quotations in critical reviews or articles, without the prior written permission of the publisher.

Published in Nashville, Tennessee, by Thomas Nelson. Thomas Nelson is a registered trademark of Thomas Nelson, Inc.

Thomas Nelson, Inc. titles may be purchased in bulk for educational, business, fundraising, or sales promotional use. For information, please e-mail SpecialMarkets@ thomasnelson.com.

Unless otherwise indicated, Scripture taken from the New Century Version. Copyright © 2005 by Thomas Nelson, Inc. Used by permission. All rights reserved.
Scripture quotations marked NIV are from the HOLY BIBLE: NEW INTERNATIONAL VERSION®. © 1973, 1978, 1984 by International Bible Society. Used by permission of Zondervan Publishing House. All rights reserved.
Scripture quotations marked MSG are from *The Message* by Eugene H. Peterson. © 1993, 1994, 1995, 1996, 2000. Used by permission of NavPress Publishing Group. All rights reserved.

Editor: Kelli B. Trujillo
Development Editors: Kelli B. Trujillo and Roxanne Wieman
Associate Editor: JoHannah Reardon
Review Editors: Marshall Shelley, David Neff
Page Designer: Robin Crosslin

ISBN-13: 978-1-4185-3423-3

Printed in the United States of America
08 09 10 11 12 RRD 6 5 4 3 2 1

CONTENTS

CONTRIBUTING WRITERS

Andy Crouch is editor of the *Christian Vision Project* (www.christianvisionproject.com).

Mark Galli is senior managing editor of *Christianity Today.*

David Goetz is founder and president of cz Marketing, author of *Death by Suburb,* and has been an editor of *Leadership Journal.*

Michael S. Horton is J. Gresham Machen Professor of Systematic Theology and Apologetics at Westminster Seminary California.

Edith M. Humphrey is professor of scripture at Augustine College, Ottawa.

Richard A. Kauffman is a former associate editor of *Christianity Today* and is now senior editor at *The Christian Century.*

Carol McLean Wilde is the author of numerous issue-based Bible studies for teens and adults.

Mark Moring is editor-at-large for *Christianity Today International.*

Ted Olson is news director and online managing editor of *Christianity Today.*

Mark I. Pinsky is a senior reporter who covers religion for *The Orlando Sentinel.*

Eric Reed is editor-in-chief of Christianity Today's Consumer Media Group.

Reid Smith is a pastor and the founder of 2orMore, a small group training and resource ministry.

John G. Stackhouse, Jr. is the Sangwoo Youtong Chee Professor of Theology and Culture at Regent College, Vancouver.

LaTonya Taylor is editorial resident at Christianity Today International.

Kelli B. Trujillo is a writer, editor, and adult ministry leader at her church.

Miroslav Volf serves as Director of the Yale Center for Faith and Culture and is the Henry B. Wright Professor of Systematic Theology at Yale Divinity School.

W. Terry Whalin is an editor and author of *Alpha's Teach Yourself the Bible in 24 Hours* (Alpha Books).

Kyle White is director of Neighbors' House, a ministry to at-risk kids in DeKalb, Illinois.

Philip Yancey is editor-at-large of *Christianity Today* and cochair of the editorial board for *Books and Culture.*

INTRODUCTION

Movies. Politics. Fashion. The Joneses. These are the forces at play in our everyday lives. They surround us, they affect us; sometimes they define us. These are the forces of our culture, but as Christians, how are we supposed to respond to culture? Ignore it? Embrace it? Run away from it? How does our faith interact with the current issues of our day? You'll explore these questions together as you examine Scripture and share from your personal experiences using this *Current Issues Bible Study* guide.

For Small Groups

These studies are designed to be used in small groups—communities of people with a commitment to and connection with each other. Whether you're an existing small group or you're just planning to meet for the next eight weeks, this resource will help you deepen your personal faith and grow closer with each other.

Along with the eight studies, you'll find a bonus Small-Group Builder article from *Christianity Today*'s SmallGroups.Com (www.smallgroups.com). On smallgroups.com, you'll find everything you need to successfully run a small-groups ministry. The insightful free articles and theme-specific downloads provide expert training. The reproducible curriculum courses bring thought leaders from across the world into your group's discussion at a fraction of the price. And the revolutionary SmallGroups Connect social network will help keep your group organized and connected 24/7.

Christianity Today Articles

Each study session begins with one or two thought-provoking articles from *Christianity Today* or one of its sister publications. These articles are meant to help you dive deeply into the topic and engage with a variety of thoughts and opinions. Be sure to read the articles before you arrive to your small group meeting; the time you invest on the front-end will greatly enrich your group's discussion. As you read, you may find the articles persuasive and agree heartily with their conclusions; other times you may disagree with the claims of an article, but that's great too. We want these articles to serve as a springboard for lively discussion, so differences in opinion are welcome.

Timing

These studies are designed to be flexible, with plenty of discussion, activities, and prayer time to fill a full small group meeting. If you'd like, you can zero in on a few questions or teaching points and discuss them in greater depth, or you can aim to spend a few minutes on each question in a given session. Be sure to manage your time so that you're able to spend time on the "Going Forward" questions and prayer time at the end of each study.

Ground Rules

True spiritual growth happens in the context of a vibrant Christian community. To establish that type of community in your small group, we recommend a few ground rules:

- Guarantee confidentiality. Promise together that whatever is said in the context of your small group meeting is kept in that small group meeting. This sense of trust and safety will enable you to more honestly share about your spiritual struggles.

- Participate—with balance. We all have different personalities. Some of us like to talk . . . a lot. Others of us prefer to be quiet. But for this study to truly benefit your group, everyone needs to participate. Make it a personal goal to answer (aloud) at least half of the discussion questions in a given session. This will allow space for others to talk (lest you dominate discussion too much) but will also guarantee your own contribution is made to the discussion (from which other group members will benefit).

- Be an attentive listener—to each other and to God. As you read Scripture and discuss these important cultural issues, focus with care and love on the other members of your group. These questions are designed to be open-ended and to allow for a diversity of opinion. Be gracious toward others who express views that are different than your own. And even more important, prayerfully remain attentive to the presence of God speaking to and guiding your group through the Holy Spirit.

It is our prayer that this *Current Issues Bible Study* guide will change the lives of your group members as you seek to integrate your faith into the cultural issues you face every day. May the Holy Spirit work in and through your group as you challenge and encourage each other in spiritual growth.

What does it really

mean to be in the

world but not of it?

SCRIPTURE FOCUS

John 3:16–21

Ephesians 4:17–5:8

CULTURE: LOVE IT, LEAVE IT, OR TRANSFORM IT

■

Some Christians fervently strive to steer clear of "the world" to the degree that they try to sanitize themselves of all things secular. Other Christians seem to embrace popular culture so much that their lives are hardly distinguishable from others around them. And then there are all the rest of Jesus' followers who fall somewhere in between these two extremes, trying to figure out what role and influence human culture should have on their way of life.

"Culture" is not a word you'll find in the Bible, though Scripture has a great deal to say about how we are to relate to the world around us. Using John G. Stackhouse, Jr.'s *Christianity Today* article "In the World, but...," we'll examine the five approaches to culture identified by H. Richard Niebuhr in his classic book, *Christ and Culture,* and we'll explore how this framework can help us discerningly engage with culture's influence in our everyday lives.

■ Before You Meet

Read "In the World, but…" by John G. Stackhouse, Jr. from *Christianity Today* magazine.

IN THE WORLD, BUT . . .

Richard Niebuhr's Christ and Culture is fifty years old— and still has something wise to say to evangelicals.

By John G. Stackhouse, Jr.

The theological world owes a great debt to Austin Presbyterian Theological Seminary in Texas, which invited Yale professor H. Richard Niebuhr to deliver the lectures that resulted in *Christ and Culture* (1951), one of the most influential Christian books of the past century. Perhaps no other book has dominated an entire theological conversation for so long. Niebuhr's famous "five types" continue to serve as the launching point for most discussions of the interaction of Christianity and culture.

To mark this fiftieth anniversary, HarperSanFrancisco has reissued *Christ and Culture* with a winsome foreword by Martin Marty, a lengthy and strangely defensive preface by ethicist James Gustafson (Niebuhr's student and friend), and a bonus essay, "Types of Christian Ethics" (1942), in which Niebuhr began to work out his analytical framework.

Like Christians of other persuasions, evangelicals have often used Niebuhr's book as a point of departure to define how we should—and should not—interact with contemporary culture. Evangelicals have inhabited all of Niebuhr's types. And, given the varied circumstances in which evangelicals have sought to serve Christ, each type can be seen to offer its own integrity—despite Niebuhr's own sometimes jaundiced view of this or that option.

Niebuhr's first type, "Christ against culture," characterizes the sectarian impulse. In "Types of Christian Ethics," Niebuhr calls this the "new law" type. Christians in this mode see the world outside the church as hopelessly corrupted by sin. The kingdom of God comes to supersede it—currently in the purity of the church, and ultimately in the messianic kingdom. God calls Christians to "come out from among them and be ye separate" in communities of holiness. Mennonites, Baptists, Christian Brethren, Pentecostals, and most types of fundamentalists have included individuals and congregations that fit this model.

At the other end of the typology lies the model of "Christ of culture," in which the absolute conflict of one against the other gives way to a harmony between them. Christians in this mode seek to discern and then champion the highest moral and spiritual common ground between the teachings of Christianity and the noblest values of contemporary culture. Niebuhr identified this model with Germany's "Culture Protestantism" of the late 19th and early 20th century, with American Whigs such as Thomas Jefferson, and with Victorian liberals such as John Stuart Mill. Evangelicals have manifested this type whenever we have closely associated God and country and assumed that our nations are Christian, or "almost," so that with enthusiasm and effort we can realize that ideal.

Three Mediating Positions

Between these two extremes lie three mediating positions. The first is "Christ above culture," the outlook of Thomas Aquinas and of many Roman Catholics ever since. In this view, all that is good in human culture is a gift from God. But to be fully realized, this good requires Christian revelation and the mediation of the church. Thus Aristotle's insights can be received joyfully by the Christian, even as they are recognized as needing Christian theology to fulfill them. Such truths as the Trinity and the Atonement are accessible only via revelation, just as the sacramental life of the church provides blessings for us that no amount of non-Christian culture can produce.

This view is uncommon among evangelicals but not altogether unknown. Consider, for example, evangelical missionaries who emphasize anticipations of Christian revelation in the beliefs of non-Christian peoples. Evangelical intellectuals who affirm the essential congeniality of the gospel with this or that non-Christian author—as the apologists of the early church allied themselves with Plato—might also fit in this category.

[handwritten margin note: what is "good"?]

[handwritten margin note: gray areas?]

The most common mediating position in evangelical circles is Niebuhr's "Christ transforming culture." Puritans in 17th-century England; Puritans in 18th-century New England; 19th-century North American revivalists trying both to evangelize and to reform society; and the late 19th-century Dutch neo-Calvinists—all of these demonstrate its traits. Society is to be entirely converted to Christianity. Business, the arts, the professions, family life, education, government—nothing is outside the purview of Christ's dominion, and all must be reclaimed in his name.

The fifth option in Niebuhr's scheme is the one that he has the most trouble making clear. He calls it "Christ and culture in paradox," and associates it with Martin Luther, Ernst Troeltsch, and (in "Types of Christian Ethics") his brother Reinhold.

In this type, Christians live within a strong tension. They believe that God has ordained worldly institutions, and that they must work within those institutions as best they can. At the same time, however, they affirm that God's kingdom has penetrated the world here and now. Thus, under God's providence, they tread a path that can seem crooked and unclear, trying to honor what is divinely ordained in culture (such as family bonds, the rule of law, and deference to legitimate authority) while also living out the distinct values of the kingdom of God as best they can without compromise.

Furthermore, sin mars all of our efforts, evil twists them, and God works in mysterious ways behind the scenes. Thus Christians in this mode are never free of suspicion yet never lacking hope: suspicion that apparently good things are compromised by sin in this not-yet-messianic dispensation, and hope that God nonetheless is working out his good pleasure through all of the means—worldly and churchly—that he has been pleased to ordain and sustain. In this in-between time, even openly evil governments may yet be instituted by God (Rom. 13:1–5); we are told to pay our taxes, though we know full well that the money will be used at least in part for ungodly purposes (Rom. 13:6–7).

It is this model of trying to cooperate with all that God is doing in the world, of bringing shalom everywhere we can while recognizing that we will rarely succeed in making only peace until Jesus returns, that North American evangelicals perhaps should consider more fully today.

Evangelicalism generally eschews paradox. We prefer the clarity of binary opposition, and there are many such pairs in the Bible: light versus darkness, good versus evil, the kingdom of God versus the kingdom of Satan, the church versus the world, the flesh versus the Spirit. Yet we are Bible people, and we must listen also to Scriptures that speak of the kingdom itself as a "mixed field" (Matt. 13:24–30), full of wheat and tares, and of the Christian life as being in the world but not of it.

Yes, we must strive for holiness, as the first type asserts. Yes, we must affirm with the second type what is genuinely good in any culture. Yes, we must rejoice in opportunities to build on good things God has already bequeathed to this or that society. And yes, we must seize every opportunity to improve, transform, and even convert this or that part of the world to the glory of God.

Yet we might also recognize that God has called us to lives of difficult paradox, of painful negotiation between conflicting and competitive values, of seeking to cooperate with God wherever he is at work. Such a position, full of ambiguity and irony, is also full of faith and hope: "in all these things we are more than conquerors" (Rom. 8:37). This is a faith that God can be trusted and honored even when the way is dark and confusing, and a hope that God works all things together for good.

John G. Stackhouse, Jr., is the Sangwoo Youtong Chee Professor of Theology and Culture at Regent College, Vancouver, Canada, and editor of No Other Gods Before Me? Evangelicals Encounter the World's Religions *(Baker Academic).*

("In the World, but…" was first published in *Christianity Today,* April 22, 2002, Vol. 46, No. 5, Page 80.)

For more insightful articles from *Christianity Today* magazine, visit http://www.ctlibrary.com/ and subscribe now.

■ Open Up

Select one of these activities to launch your discussion time.

Option 1

Discuss one of these icebreaker questions:

- Name one of your favorite TV shows, movies, or songs. What do you like about it? *NUMB3RS*

  The scientific (mathematical) approach to solving crimes.

- Now name a TV show, movie, or song you know of that you think represents some of the worst aspects of our culture. What *don't* you like about it?

  We now have Direct TV. It includes 3 free months of HBO which we would not pay for. A sample we looked at was Harry Potter. Lots of discussion there. A second feature showed sexual comments and was crude. (Turned it off)

- Think through a typical day in your life. In what way does our culture (its values, trends, etc.) intersect with your daily life? Brainstorm together as many intersections that occur in an average day as you can.

Option 2

Together watch a short clip from a popular TV show that in some way reflects non-Christian values.

- Read the statements below. Which one best reflects your response to TV shows like this one? Why?

Old "Roseann" show. "No ChristianValue"

1. Christians simply shouldn't watch programs like this.

2. Christians should do what they can to try to influence programming by pressuring TV networks to offer more family-friendly shows or by boycotting advertisers.

3. Christians should get involved in the secular entertainment business themselves in order to try to influence it for good.

4. Christians cannot influence the secular entertainment world; rather, they should create alternative programming and/or networks.

5. Christians should watch these programs together and discuss them, asking themselves what they say about human nature and longing. Or parents should watch these programs with their children and talk about the value conflicts they pose for Christians.

6. These programs really aren't so bad; it's just entertainment describing the lives of real people, after all.

■ The Issue

Christians cannot be Christian, nor can the church be the church, without some tension with the world and its cultures. How should we approach the culture in which we live? Should we embrace it? Reject it? Or something in between?

Stackhouse's article "In the World, but…" explores the five different stances on this issue that H. Richard Niebuhr identified in his classic work *Christ and Culture*:

1. Christ against culture
2. Christ above culture
3. Christ transforming culture
4. Christ and culture in paradox
5. Christ of culture

- As you read "In the World, but…", which of Niebuhr's approaches toward culture did you most identify with? Why?

  #4 - It seems to reflect what is actually happening today.

- Which did you least identify with? Why?

  #1 Christ against culture. It tends to build up walls between people, families, even spouses.

■ Reflect

Take a moment to read John 3:16–21 and Ephesians 4:17–5:8 on your own. Jot down a few notes and observations about the passages: What stands out to you most? In what ways do you think these passages speak to the way we should view culture? What questions or issues do these passages bring up?

God does not give us any "gray areas" for how we should conduct ourselves. It's all "black or white".

■ Let's Explore

God loves the world in spite of its evil.

- When you think about our culture, do you generally tend to focus on the things God loves in it or the things God hates in it? Why?

Our culture is slipping out of the "God loves category" into the "God hates category"

- Read John 3:16–18. "For God so loved the world," the first phrase in this passage, is so familiar that we may take its meaning for granted. What does this phrase mean? What do you think "the world" refers to here?

God loved the whole world in spite of its sinful nature. Jesus came so that the whole world would have a choice. Either accept Christ or reject Christ. (no gray area)

- Consider the five approaches to culture that Niebuhr identifies. How might people with these varying perspectives understand the phrase "For God so loved the world" differently?

When God loved the world, He did it unconditionally so the world had a new start spiritually with Jesus. Most rejected Jesus.

Christians are called to influence the world (culture) as salt and light.

- Read Matthew 5:13–16 aloud. Now read both John 3:16–18 and Matthew 5:13–16 aloud again, but this time insert the word "culture" wherever "earth" or "world" appears. What is your reaction to this re-casting of the passage? Do you think this altered perspective accurately reflects God's stance toward human culture and our role in it? Why or why not?

① It does not accurately reflect the totality of God's love.
② God's love cannot be limited by man's attempt to organise the world.
③ God's love will always be totally inclusive of all of mankind.

- Examine Ephesians 4:17—5:8. Which of these instructions for Christian living jump out to you as powerful ways to be salt and light? How could living in this way impact the culture? When have you observed examples of this?

4:29 Watch your mouth. You can build up or tear down a person just by what you say.
Walk in the light and people will see the light in you.

- In what concrete ways do you see Christians serve as salt within our culture? Where in our culture are Christians serving as light, dispelling the darkness?

We need Christians in the courts of the land. We need Christians in law enforcements.

The sin and evil in our culture demand a discerning response from us.

- The strength of the Christ-against-culture view is that it reminds us that evil is a dark reality in this world and that as God's holy people we should flee from it. Read John 3:19–21 and review Ephesians 4:17–19. What are some examples of "darkness" and "evil" in our culture that immediately come to mind?

The drugs and sex businesses are totally in the dark

- How does your stance towards the aspects of culture you consider to be obviously dark or evil compare with your approach toward aspects of culture that aren't quite as "bad"?

God doesn't offer us shades of gray in our relationship with him.

In his exploration of the "Christ and Culture in paradox" stance, Stackhouse claims that paradox is a difficult and uncomfortable place for evangelicals to occupy. He says, "We prefer the clarity of binary opposition, and there are many such pairs in the Bible: light versus darkness, good versus evil, the kingdom of God versus the kingdom of Satan, the church versus the world, the flesh versus the Spirit."

But Stackhouse himself seems to prefer this "Christ and culture in paradox" position, concluding that "we might also recognize that God has called us to lives of difficult paradox, of painful negotiation between conflicting and competitive values, of seeking to cooperate with God wherever he is at work. Such a position, full of ambiguity and irony, is also full of faith and hope: 'in all these things we are more than conquerors' (Romans 8:37). This is a faith that God can be trusted and honored even when the way is dark and confusing, and a hope that God works all things together for good."

- Describe a recent instance in your own life when you were forced to make a moral decision in which there were not obvious "black and white" alternatives, only different shades of gray? How did you discern what you should do?

In a trenchant critique of Niebuhr's *Christ and Culture* typology, John Howard Yoder argues that culture isn't monolithic. Even the Amish, for example, aren't anti-culture; they accept some aspects of the dominant culture while developing alternatives for other aspects. Some aspects of any given culture Christians will be able to use and accept; others, they will need to reject. This calls for discernment that takes place in the context of the church, the body of Christ, informed by Scripture under the guidance of the Holy Spirit. This discernment will lead Christians to reject some aspects of culture, adopt and adapt other aspects, and work toward the transformation of still other elements of culture.

- Where do you draw the line between aspects of culture Christians should flee from and parts of culture they can embrace or enjoy? What elements of our culture do you think Christians should seek to transform?

Flee from drugs, sex, illigal money schemes.
Embrace classical music, art in all its Godly forms.

■ Going Forward

It can be very easy to get into the habit of approaching culture on "autopilot"—making decisions about how we respond to it simply based on habit or personal taste. But God desires us to take these choices very seriously—to seek his will and to be guided by the Holy Spirit.

Break into pairs to discuss these final questions:

- How often do you approach culture on "autopilot"? In what ways do you feel God wants you to be more discerning about your engagement with culture? Be specific.

- What's one area of your life in which you sense God prompting you to take your role as salt and light more seriously? How will you do that?

Pray for your partner, specifically addressing the areas in which you each feel challenged to grow. Then take turns reading Philippians 1:9–11 aloud as part of your prayer for each other.

■ Want to Explore More?

Recommended Resources

Authentic Transformation: A New Vision of Christ and Culture; Glen H. Stassen, D. M. Yeager, and John Howard Yoder (Abingdon Press, 1996; ISBN 0687022738)

Christ and Culture Revisited, D.A. Carson (Wm. B. Eerdmans Publishing Company, 2008; ISBN 0802831745)

Christ and Culture, H. Richard Niebuhr (HarperCollins, 2001; ISBN 0061300039)

Resident Aliens: Life in the Christian Colony, Stanley Hauerwas and William H. Willimon (Abingdon Press, 1989; ISBN 0687361591)

Rethinking Christ and Culture: A Post-Christendom Perspective, Craig A. Carter (Brazos, 2007; ISBN 1587431599)

"With or Against Culture" Jean Bethke Elshtain and other articles in the "Culture" section of The Christian Vision Project Web site: www.christianvisionproject.com/2006_culture

■ Notes

What does it look like

to live as citizens of

God's present-and-future

kingdom?

SCRIPTURE FOCUS

Matthew 5:1–12, 13:24–33

Philippians 3:17–4:1

KINGDOM-MINDED
LIVING IN THE KINGDOM
OF THIS WORLD

■

When Michael S. Horton looks at American evangelicalism, he sees a tradition whose global positioning system is out of whack. "Instead of being in the world but not of it," he writes, "we easily become of the world but not in it." As a result of this error, the church and society both suffer.

What is God's kingdom supposed to look like? How does our citizenship in that kingdom influence the way we relate to our culture? We'll use Horton's *Christianity Today* article "How the Kingdom Comes" as a starting point for discussion about these and other important questions.

■ Before You Meet

Read "How the Kingdom Comes" by Michael S. Horton from *Christianity Today* magazine.

HOW THE KINGDOM COMES

The church becomes countercultural not by what it gives, but by what it gets.

By Michael S. Horton WORDS - Pg. 39

It was confusing to grow up singing both "This World Is Not My Home" and "This Is My Father's World." Those hymns embody two common and seemingly contradictory Christian responses to culture. One sees this world as a wasteland of godlessness, with which the Christian should have as little as possible to do. The other regards cultural transformation as virtually identical to "kingdom activity."

Certainly the answer does not lie in any intrinsic opposition of heaven and earth. After all, Jesus taught us to pray, "Your kingdom come, your will be done on earth as it is in heaven." Rather, the answer is to be sought in understanding the particular moment in redemptive history where God has placed us. We are not yet in the Promised Land, where the kingdom of God may be directly identified with earthly kingdoms and cultural pursuits. Yet we are no longer in Egypt. We are pilgrims in between, on the way.

In Babylon, God commanded the exiles to "build houses and settle down," pursuing the good of their conquering neighbors (Jer. 29). At the same time, he prophesied a new city, an everlasting empire, as the true homeland that would surpass anything Israel had experienced in Canaan.

So both of my childhood hymns tell the truth in their own way: We are pilgrims and strangers in this age, but we "pass through" to the age to come (not some ethereal state of spiritual bliss), which, even now in this present evil age, is dawning.

The challenge is to know what time it is, what the kingdom is, how it comes, and where we should find it right now.

Is Christianity a Culture?

In the Old Covenant, the kingdom of God was identified with the nation of Israel, anticipating the Last Day by executing on a small scale the judgment and blessings that will come one day to the whole world. Yet Jesus introduced a different policy with the new covenant. Instead of calling on God's people to drive out the Canaanites in holy war, Jesus pointed out that God blesses both believers and unbelievers. He expects his people to love and serve rather than judge and condemn their neighbors, even their enemies (Matt. 5:43–48; see also Matt. 7:1–6). The wheat and the weeds are to be allowed to grow together, separated only at the final harvest (Matt. 13:24–30). The kingdom at present is hidden under suffering and the Cross, conquering through Word and sacrament, yet one day it will be consummated as a kingdom of glory and power. First the Cross, weakness, and suffering; then glory, power, and the announcement that the kingdoms of this world have been made the kingdom of Christ (Rev. 11:15; see also Heb. 2:5–18).

So what is the relationship of Christians to culture in this time between the times? Is Jesus Christ Lord over secular powers and principalities? At least in Reformed theology, the answer is yes, though he is Lord in different ways over the world and the church. God presently rules the world through providence and common grace, while he rules the church through Word, sacrament, and covenantal nurture.

This means that there is no difference between Christians and non-Christians with respect to their vocations. "We urge you, brothers, to [love one another] more and more," Paul writes. "Make it your ambition to lead a quiet life, to mind your own business, and to work with your hands, just as we told you, so that your daily life may win the respect of outsiders and so that you will not be dependent on anybody" (1 Thess. 4:10–12 NIV). There are no calls in the New Testament either to withdraw into a private ghetto or to "take back" the realms of cultural and political activity. Rather, we find exhortations, like Paul's, to the inauspicious yet crucial task of loving and serving our neighbors with excellence. Until Christ returns, believers will share with unbelievers in pain and pleasure, poverty and wealth, hurricanes and holidays. A believer, however, will not be anxious about the future and will not "grieve like the rest of men, who have no hope," as Paul adds (1 Thess. 4:13 NIV), but will be energized in the most mundane daily pursuits by the knowledge that God will raise the dead and set everything right (1 Thess. 4:14–18). We groan inwardly for that final redemption with the whole of creation, precisely because we already have within us the Spirit as a down payment and guarantee (Rom. 8:18–25).

The earthly citizenship to which Jesus, Paul, and Peter referred is therefore a common sphere for believers and unbelievers. The second-century *Epistle to Diognetus* offers a self-portrait of the early Christian community:

For Christians are distinguished from the rest of men neither by country nor by language nor by customs. For nowhere do they dwell in cities of their own; they do not use any strange form of speech. . . But while they dwell in both Greek and barbarian cities, each as his lot was cast, and follow the customs of the land in dress and food and other matters of living, they show forth the remarkable and admittedly strange order of their own citizenship. They live in fatherlands of their own, but as aliens. They share all things as citizens and suffer all things as strangers. Every foreign land is their fatherland, and every fatherland a foreign land. . . . They pass their days on earth, but they have their citizenship in heaven.

So Christians are not called to make holy apparel, speak an odd dialect of spiritual jargon, or transform their workplace, neighborhood, or nation into the kingdom of Christ. Rather, they are called to belong to a holy commonwealth that is distinct from the regimes of this age (Phil. 3:20–21) and to contribute as citizens and neighbors in temporal affairs. "For here we do not have an enduring city, but we are looking for the city that is to come" (Heb. 13:14 NIV). The church, therefore, as the communion of saints gathered by God for preaching, teaching, sacrament, prayer, and fellowship (Acts 2:46–47), is distinct from the broader cultural activities to which Christians are called in love and service to their neighbors. In our day, this pattern is often reversed, creating a pseudo-Christian subculture that fails to take either calling seriously.

Instead of being in the world but not of it, we easily become of the world but not in it.

But the church is not really a culture. The kingdom of God is never something that we bring into being, but something that we are receiving. Cultural advances occur by concentrated and collective effort, while the kingdom of God comes to us through baptism, preaching, teaching, Eucharist, prayer, and fellowship. "Therefore, since we are receiving a kingdom that cannot be shaken, let us be thankful, and so worship God acceptably with reverence and awe, for our 'God is a consuming fire'" (Heb. 12:28–29 NIV). There is nothing more important for the church than to receive and proclaim the kingdom in joyful assembly, raising children in the covenant of grace. They are heirs with us of that future place for those "who have tasted the heavenly gift, who have shared in the Holy Spirit, who have tasted the goodness of the Word of God and the powers of the coming age"—a holy land "which drinks in the rain often falling on it" and is "farmed" so that it reaps its Sabbath blessing (Heb. 6:4–8 NIV).

A Counterculture?

If the church is not to be identified with culture, is it necessarily a counterculture? If Christians as well as non-Christians participate in the common curse and common grace of this age in secular affairs, then there is no "Christian politics" or "Christian art" or "Christian literature," any more than there is "Christian plumbing." The church has no authority to bind Christian (much less non-Christian) consciences beyond Scripture. When it does, the church as "counterculture" is really just another subculture, an auxiliary of one faction of the current culture wars, distracted from its proper ministry of witnessing to Christ and the new society that he is forming around himself (Gal. 3:26–29). This new society neither ignores nor is consumed by the cultural conflicts of the day.

Recently, an older pastor told me that during the Vietnam era, two of his parishioners, one a war protestor and the other a veteran, were embroiled in a debate in the parking lot, but then joined each other at the Communion rail with their arms around each other. Here was a witness to the Sabbath rest that awaits us, realizing that we still have, for the time being, vineyards to plant and wars to be for or against as citizens.

Too often, of course, the contemporary church simply mirrors the culture. Increasingly, we are less a holy city drawn together around Christ and more a part of the suburban sprawl that celebrates individual autonomy, choice, entertainment, and pragmatic efficiency. These are values that can build highways and commerce, but they cannot sustain significant bonds across cultural divides and between generations. Capitulating to niche demographics and marketing, churches that once nurtured the young, middle-aged, and elderly together, with all of the indispensable gifts that each one brings to the body of Christ, often now contribute to the rending of this intergenerational fabric. If this is a worrisome trend in the social sphere, it is all the more troubling for a body that is constituted by its Lord as a covenantal community.

To be truly countercultural, the church must first receive and then witness to Peter's claim in Acts 2:39: "The promise is for you and your children and for all who are far off—for all whom the Lord our God will call" (NIV). The promise is not only for us, but also for our children. According to recent studies by sociologists like Christian Smith, evangelical teens are only slightly less likely than their unchurched friends to adopt a working creed of "moralistic, therapeutic deism." As the diet in our churches is increasingly determined by the spirit of the age, and as youth are treated as borderline cases to be cajoled into thinking God is cool, the church risks abandoning that promise. The "pumped-up" teens in our youth groups today are often tomorrow's skeptics and burnouts. They don't need more hip Christian slogans, T-shirts, and other subcultural distractions, but the means of grace for maturing into co-heirs with Christ.

Recently, CNN reporter Anderson Cooper was asked, "Do you think part of your job is to appeal to younger viewers?" "I've never been in a meeting where people said to bring in younger people," he replied. "I think the notion of telling stories differently to appeal to younger people is a mistake. Young people want the same kind of thing older viewers do: interesting, well-told, compelling stories. If you're somehow altering what you're doing because you want to get young viewers, that's a little bit like when your parents go out to buy 'cool' clothes for you." In our culture, relevance is determined—in fact, created—by publicity. But the Word creates its own publicity as it is preached, as the story is told. It creates its own relevance, and as a result, a community that spans the generations.

Let God's Word work!

The promise is not only for us and for our children, Peter says, but "for all who are far off—for all whom the Lord our God will call" (Acts 2:39 NIV). And how does he call them? Through the preaching of the gospel. Peter's promise, in fact, is part of such a sermon, proclaiming Christ as the center of Scripture. Refusing to set a covenantal church ("you and your children") against a missional church ("all who are far off"), the apostolic community stuck to its calling and became both an outpost and lightning rod for God's saving activity in the world.

If ours is to truly be a countercultural community, it must begin with the rejection of any notion of self-founding, either in creation or redemption. It is God's choice, not ours; God's "planned community," not ours; God's means of grace, not our ambitious programs, plans, or achievements that extend the kingdom. Being "countercultural" today often amounts to superficial moralism about sex and SUVs, or perhaps creating wholesome novels with Christian heroes, removing offensive language from music lyrics, and encouraging positive values. Beyond that, many of the churches with which I am familiar are captivated by the same obsessions as our culture: religion as individual spirituality, therapy, and sentimentalism. It all serves to keep us turned in on ourselves, like a kid at a carnival instead of a pilgrim en route.

Describing the rapid decline of rural areas that are surrendering to strip malls and homogeneous multinational corporations, Wendell Berry argues, "We must learn to grow like a tree, not like a fire." Berry notes that we are losing our ability to take any place seriously, since this demands patience, love, study, and hard work—in other words, roots. Some use the word "seekers" to describe those we are trying to reach in this culture. But the truth is that they and we are more like tourists than seekers, let alone pilgrims, flying from place to place to consume experiences.

Can churches be a counterculture amidst anonymous neighborhoods and tourist destinations, the apotheoses of individual choice, niche demographics, and marketing? Yes. The church can exist amidst suburban sprawl as easily as in cities or small towns, precisely because its existence is determined by the realities of the age to come—by God's work, rather than by the narrow possibilities of our work in this present age under sin and death. After all, this is our Father's world, even though, for the moment, we are just passing through.

Michael S. Horton is J. Gresham Machen Professor of Systematic Theology and Apologetics at Westminster Seminary California.

("How the Kingdom Comes" was first published in *Christianity Today*, January 2006, Vol. 50, No. 1, Page 42)

For more insightful articles from *Christianity Today* magazine, visit http://www.ctlibrary.com/ and subscribe now.

■ Open Up

Select one of these activities to launch your discussion time.

Option 1

Discuss one of these icebreaker questions:

• Where do you feel most "at home" in your house? What's your favorite spot to hang out in? Why?

- Now, excluding your literal home, in what other places or situations do you feel most "at home"? (Such as a favorite coffee shop, enjoying a hobby, or spending time with a particular group of friends.) Why?

Option 2

Write the name of each group member on a slip of paper, then shuffle the slips and redistribute them. (Make sure no one draws his or her own name.) Now, with paper and pencil in hand, spread out around your meeting area and quickly draw a sketch of the person whose name you received. Take just 1 minute to create your portrait.

When 1 minute is up, gather all the drawings together. Hold them up, one at a time, and try to guess as a group who the drawing is supposed to represent.

Then talk about these questions:

- Which physical traits in the portraits were the most recognizable? Why?

- What are some traits that you think should make Christians recognizable in our culture? Why?

■ The Issue

In his article "How the Kingdom Comes," Michael S. Horton writes, "Instead of being in the world, but not of it, we easily become of the world but not in it."

- How would you define these two phrases: "in the world" and "of the world"?

- Do you agree with Horton's assertion? If so, what examples come to mind for you of Christians who seem to be of the world but not in it? If you don't agree with Horton, why not?

■ Reflect

Take a moment to read Matthew 5:1–12, 13:24–33 and Philippians 3:17–4:1 on your own. Jot down a few notes and observations about the passages: What insights do these passages give you about the kingdom of God? Which images, words, or phrases stand out to you the most? What questions do you have about these passages?

■ Let's Explore

We are pilgrims—not tourists—in this world.

Horton begins his article by talking about two traditional Christian songs: "This World Is Not My Home" and "This Is My Father's World." For Horton, these songs exemplify two very different Christian responses to culture.

Consider these lyrics from the two songs:

"This world is not my home, I'm just-a-passing through.
My pleasure and my hopes are placed beyond the blue.
. . . And I can't feel at home in this world anymore."

("This World Is Not My Home")

"This is my Father's world: He shines in all that's fair;
In the rustling grass I hear Him pass;
He speaks to me everywhere.
This is my Father's World. O let me ne'er forget
That though the wrong seems oft so strong, God is the ruler yet.
. . . This is my Father's world, a wanderer I may roam
Whate'er my lot, it matters not.
My heart is still at home."

("This Is My Father's World")

• Which lines from these song lyrics stand out to you? Which song do you relate to more? Why?

- Read Philippians 3:17–4:1. Here Paul admonishes the Philippian Christians to focus on their citizenship in heaven, firmly fixing their gaze ahead. Horton captures this idea by saying, "We are pilgrims in between, on the way." What do you think it means to live as a pilgrim? Explain.

- Horton critiques modern Christians, saying we are more like "tourists" than pilgrims, "flying from place to place to consume experiences." How would you define the difference between a tourist mind-set and a pilgrim mind-set? In what ways have you seen Christians relate to this world as tourists?

As pilgrims, we are to focus our eyes on the kingdom of God that will be fulfilled in the future, as Paul admonishes in Philippians 3:20. But Mark records the beginning of Jesus' ministry with these words: "Jesus went into Galilee, proclaiming the good news of God. 'The time has come,' he said. 'The kingdom of God is near. Repent and believe the good news!'" (Mark 1:14–15 NIV)

Over and over again in the Gospels, Jesus asserts that the kingdom of God is "near" or is "at hand." This is not future tense language but *present tense*. Embodied in Jesus, explained in his teachings, and at work in his church, the kingdom of God is a present part of our lives here on this earth. Followers of Christ are citizens of that kingdom (Colossians 1:12–13) in the here and now, not just the future. Dutch theologian Geerhardus Vos described this dual nature of the kingdom as being both "already" and "not yet." As John Bright aptly puts it in *The Kingdom of God,* "The Kingdom of God . . . has come and is even now in the world; it is also yet to come. In the tension between the two, the Church must live."

In his book *The Upside-Down Kingdom*, author Donald B. Kraybill uses an analogy quite different than pilgrimage to describe the way Christians are to live in this world. He writes, "Jesus does not portray the kingdom on the margins of society. He doesn't plead for social avoidance or withdrawal. Nor does he assume that the kingdom and the world split neatly into two separate realms. Kingdom action takes place in the world in the middle of the societal ballpark. But it's a different game. Kingdom players follow special rules and heed another coach."

- What's your response to this sports imagery? What additional insights does it offer about what it means to be part of the kingdom of God "team"? In addition to pilgrim or kingdom player, what other word pictures or analogies can you think of that describe what our role in this world should be?

We are to live in *this world—not in a holy "ghetto."*

In Matthew 13, Jesus uses seven different parables to explain the relationship between the kingdom of God (and its citizens) and the world. Read three of these parables, found in Matthew 13:24–33.

- How do Jesus's parables of the weeds, the mustard seed, and the yeast shed light on what it means to be "in this world"? What do these parables reveal about the church's mission in this world?

Horton mentions the tendency of some Christians to "withdraw into a private ghetto" or to create and live in a "pseudo-Christian subculture." He particularly decries the way Christian subculture is used to lure teens toward Christian faith, saying "[Y]outh are treated as borderline cases to be cajoled into thinking God is cool. . . . .They don't need more hip Christian slogans, T-shirts, and other subcultural distractions, but the means of grace for maturing into co-heirs with Christ."

- Do you think the growing Christian subculture—exemplified in Christian music, Christian fiction, Christian movies, Christian lingo, Christian T-shirts, Christian jewelry, and so on—is equivalent to withdrawing from the world into a private "ghetto"? Why or why not?

- How can these aspects of Christian subculture be "distractions" from living out a kingdom mind-set? Or, alternately, how can they benefit our faith? Share from your own experience.

Our lives are to mirror the values of the kingdom—not the culture.

Jesus had much to say about the kingdom of God (or "the kingdom of heaven"), particularly in the Sermon on the Mount, which has been called his "inauguration manifesto" for the kingdom. Here, beginning with the Beatitudes, Jesus powerfully reveals how completely different the values of God's kingdom are from the values of this world. Read Matthew 5:1–12.

- What stands out to you most from Jesus's words here? Which values of our current culture do these kingdom values butt up against? Share specific examples.

- In addition to his teachings, Jesus's actions also reveal the values of the kingdom. What are some other teachings or actions of Jesus that reveal kingdom values in stark contrast with the values of our culture?

A key argument of Horton's article is the claim that often "the contemporary church simply mirrors the culture." Horton points out that when we are different from the culture, it is usually in all the wrong ways: "Being 'countercultural' today often amounts to superficial moralism about sex and SUVs, or perhaps creating wholesome novels with Christian heroes, removing offensive language from music lyrics, and encouraging positive values." He goes on to say that instead he's observed many Christians who "are captivated by the same obsessions as our culture: religion as individual spirituality, therapy, and sentimentalism."

- Do you agree with Horton's critique? Why or why not? If so, in what ways have you seen contemporary culture mirrored in the church? Or how have you seen the church model kingdom values in contrast with the culture's values?

■ Going Forward

Break into pairs to discuss this next question:

- Revisit Horton's assertion that "Instead of being in the world, but not of it, we easily become of the world but not in it." Which do you tend to struggle with more: The tendency to embrace and mirror cultural trends and values (being "of" the world)? Or the tendency toward Christian isolationism (not living "in" the world)? Why?

Gather back together as a group to talk about this final question:

- In *The Upside-Down Kingdom*, Kraybill writes, "Kingdom values challenge the taken-for-granted social ruts and sometimes run against the dominant cultural grain." Based on your discussion of kingdom values, what's one specific way you feel challenged to boldly live "against the dominant cultural grain"?

Pray the Lord's Prayer as a group, pausing after the phrase "thy kingdom come" to allow each group member to add a personal reflection about the kingdom of God, silently or aloud.

■ Want to Explore More?

Recommended Resources

Soul Searching: The Religious and Spiritual Lives of American Teenagers, Christian Smith and Melinda Lundquist Denton (Oxford, 2005; ISBN 019518095X)

The Church in Emerging Culture: Five Perspectives, Leonard Sweet, ed. (Zondervan, 2003; ISBN 0310254876)

The Gospel of the Kingdom, George Eldon Ladd (Wm. B. Eerdmans Publishing Company, 1959; ISBN 0802812805)

The Kingdom of God, John Bright (Abingdon Press, 1981; ISBN 0687209080)

The Kingdom of God, Martyn Lloyd-Jones (Crossway Books, 1992; ISBN 0891076484)

The Upside-Down Kingdom, Donald S. Kraybill (Herald Press, 2003; ISBN 0836192362)

Where in the World Is the Church? Michael S. Horton (P&R Publishing, 2002; ISBN 0875525652)

Do you have an answer

for the misconceptions

about Christianity?

SCRIPTURE FOCUS

2 Corinthians 4:1–6

1 Peter 3:13–16

ANSWER THE SKEPTICS

■

Newspaper and magazine articles regularly report the growing influence of evangelicals, a term perceived by the public as a catch-all religious phrase for someone who is a fanatic. The stories are often related to issues in the political arena or the economic buying power of Christians. How do you engage your skeptical (or hostile) neighbor or coworker who is not a Christian with the Good News about Jesus Christ? While people who appreciate the man Jesus may not be hard to find, skeptics who react to the word *Christian* seem to be everywhere.

Using Philip Yancey's *Christianity Today* article "Exploring a Parallel Universe," we'll look at the issues surrounding the skepticism about Christianity and think through the necessity of giving a good answer for our faith.

(margin handwriting: How often did we forum an opinion w/ thout having all the facts on both sides?)

(margin handwriting: How little gov't could the country survive on?)

■ Before You Meet

Read "Exploring a Parallel Universe" by Philip Yancey from *Christianity Today* magazine.

EXPLORING A PARALLEL UNIVERSE

Why does the word evangelical *threaten so many people in our culture?*

by Philip Yancey, for the study, "Answer the Skeptics"

For almost ten years, I have participated in a book group comprising people who attended the University of Chicago. Mostly we read current novels, with a preference for those authors (Philip Roth, Saul Bellow, J. M. Coetzee) who have a connection with the school. The group includes a Marxist-leaning professor of philosophy, a childhood-development specialist, a pharmaceutical researcher, a neurologist, and an attorney.

I marvel in our meetings at how the same book can evoke radically different responses. Yet after navigating a sea of ideas, the living room conversations almost always drift back to political issues. Though I live in a red state, all but one of my book buddies are liberal Democrats—the sole exception being a libertarian who opposes nearly all government.

The group views me as a window to a parallel universe. "You know evangelicals, right?" I nod yes. "Can you explain to us why they are so opposed to homosexuals getting married?" I do my best, but the arguments I cite from leading evangelicals make little sense to this group.

After the 2004 election, the Marxist professor launched into a tirade against "right-wing evangelicals." "They're motivated by hate—sheer hate!" he said. I suggested fear as a possible alternative, fear of changes in a society that is moving in a troubling direction. "No, it's hate!" he insisted, uncharacteristically raising his voice and turning red in the face.

"Do you personally know any 'right-wing evangelicals'?" I asked. "Not really," he admitted a little sheepishly, though he said he had known many in his youth.

I have learned from this group how threatening religion can seem, especially to those who see themselves as a minority of agnostics in a land of belief. They tend to regard evangelicals as moral police determined to impose their ideas of proper behavior on people who do not share their beliefs. *ANY CHURCH COULD FALL INTO THAT TRAP!*

Visiting another city a few months ago, I met with three gay men who consider themselves Christians, attend church regularly, and take their faith seriously. They view the political landscape through the same lens as my reading group friends, though with a far more acute sense of alarm. "We feel like we're in the same situation as the Jews in the early days of Hitler's regime," said one. "We're trying to discern whether it's 1933 or 1939. Should we all flee to Canada now? It's obvious the country doesn't want us, and I believe most evangelicals would like to see us exterminated." *IT WOULD BE EASY FOR THE MINORITY TO ASSUME THE WORST.*

I responded with sheer incredulity. "How can you think such a thing! Homosexuals have more rights in this country than ever. And I don't know a single Christian who wants to have you exterminated." The three cited legislative efforts in several states to roll back rights granted homosexuals and gave me several pages of inflammatory rhetoric against homosexuals by prominent evangelical political activists.

I went away from that discussion with my head spinning, just as sometimes happens at the university reading group. How can people who inhabit the same society have such different perceptions? More ominously, what have we evangelicals done to make Good News—the very meaning of the word *evangelical*—sound like such a threat?

Only one person in the reading group has expressed interest in matters of faith. One evening Josh told us about his sister, now a conservative evangelical. She had been a drug addict, unable to hold a job or keep a marriage together. "Then one day she found Jesus," Josh said. "There's no other explanation. She changed from night to day."

Josh asked me to recommend some books by C. S. Lewis or someone else who could explain the faith in a way that he could understand. "My sister sends me Christian books, but they're totally unconvincing," he said. "They seem written for people who already believe them." I happily complied. *C.S. LEWIS' COMMENT ABOUT COURTING A VIRGIN VS. ONE WHO HAD PREVIOUSLY BEEN MARRIED.*

Reflecting on our conversation, I remembered a remark by Lewis, who drew a distinction between communicating with a society that hears the gospel for the first time and one that has embraced and then largely rejected it. A person must court a virgin differently than a divorcée, said Lewis. One welcomes the charming words; the other needs a demonstration of love to overcome inbuilt skepticism.

I thought, too, how tempting it can be—and how distracting from our primary mission—to devote so many efforts to rehabilitating society at large, especially when these efforts demonize the opposition. (After all, neither Jesus nor Paul showed much concern about cleaning up the degenerate Roman Empire.) As history has proven, especially in times when church and state closely mingle, it is possible for the church to gain a nation and in the process lose the kingdom.

Philip Yancey is editor at large of Christianity Today and cochair of the editorial board for Books and Culture.

("Exploring a Parallel Universe," by Philip Yancey, was first published in *Christianity Today*, November 2005, Page 128.)

For more insightful articles from *Christianity Today* magazine, visit http://www.ctlibrary.com/ and subscribe now.

■ Open Up

Select one of these activities to launch your discussion time.

Option 1

Discuss one of these icebreaker questions:

• Think back to the time you first met one of your close friends. What were your first impressions? What attracted you to him or her?

- Now think of someone you don't like very much. Without giving the person's name, what are some of that person's characteristics that really put you off? What judgments have you formed—right or wrong—about that person?

How about a friend who has changed as I have and we never discuss our differences.?

Option 2

We all tend to label other people—and others label us as well. Grab three index cards and write down three labels others might "stick" on you, one per card (for example, "father," "accountant," "teacher). Don't include your name on the cards.

Shuffle everyone's cards together, then take turns each drawing a card and guessing who wrote it. When you're done, discuss:

- How accurately do these labels describe us?

I like this! Maybe we could do this in the home group we just joined after 6 mos of being together.

■ The Issue

In "Exploring a Parallel Universe," Yancey describes how religious views threaten those individuals who view "themselves as a minority of agnostics in a land of belief." Because they only read about evangelicals instead of knowing them personally, "they tend to regard evangelicals as morals police determined to impose their ideas of proper behavior on people who do not share their beliefs."

- How is the label *evangelical* tossed around in conversations or the news media? Can you describe when you have seen or felt these misconceptions personally?

THE TERM "EVANGELICAL" IS USUALLY TIED TO SOME NEGATIVE CONNOTATION BY THE MEDIA. THE MEDIA CONSISTANTLY THROWS OUT LABELS. OF COURSE ALL OF US CAN BE GUILTY OCCASIONALLY.

■ Reflect

Take a moment to read 2 Corinthians 4:1–6 and 1 Peter 3:13–16 on your own. Jot down a few notes and observations about the passages: What stands out to you most? What similar themes or ideas do you see in these passages? What questions do these passages bring up?

2 COR 4:1-6 - IN SPITE OF ALL THE DARKNESS AROUND US, WE ARE CALLED TO REFLECT THE LIGHT OF JESUS WHEREVER WE ARE.

■ Let's Explore

It is healthy for our own spiritual life to befriend non-Christians.

From the early days of his earthly ministry, Jesus Christ confounded the expectations of the religious leaders and made friendships with unexpected people. When criticized for his choices in companions, Jesus said in Luke 5:31, "It is not the healthy who need a doctor, but the sick (NIV)." Yet numerous Christians isolate themselves and make friends only with those who mirror their beliefs.

- Why do you think many Christians end up isolated—without any meaningful relationships with non-Christians? Is it wrong to live like that? Why or why not?

- In 1 Peter 2:12, Peter admonishes "Live such good lives among the pagans that . . . they may see your good deeds and glorify God (NIV)." 1 Peter 3:13–16 and 2 Corinthians 4:1–6 also emphasize the importance of living an exemplary life in order to point non-Christians toward Jesus. Re-read these passages, then discuss this question: How can relationships with non-Christians keep us on our toes, so to speak?

- Take a moment to evaluate your life through the eyes of others. What are the outward evidences of a changed life in Christ? How does your life offer hope or defy labels and stereotypes?

- How have relationships or encounters you've had with non-Christians benefited your faith and challenged you to grow? Share a specific area in which you've felt challenged.

Prepare for unexpected conversations so that you can seize opportunities to talk about your faith in Christ.

- Where do you feel most comfortable talking about your faith? Where do you feel least comfortable?

- Re-read 1 Peter 3:15–16. When has an opportunity to speak about faith snuck up on you, unexpected? Did you feel prepared? What happened?

- What do you think is the most effective way for a person to talk about their faith? What insights do 1 Peter 3:15–16 and 2 Corinthians 4:2, 5 provide?

- On the flip side, what approaches do you think are generally least effective? Why?

Love is the overriding force to demonstrate Jesus to skeptics.

Near the conclusion of Yancey's article, he recalls a remark from C.S. Lewis, "who drew a distinction between communicating with a society that hears the gospel for the first time and one that has embraced and then largely rejected it. A person must court a virgin differently than a divorcée, said Lewis. One welcomes the charming words; the other needs a demonstration of love to overcome inbuilt skepticism."

- Consider this comparison of someone who does not believe in Christ to either a virgin or a divorcée. How have you experienced these differences in conversations with non-Christian friends (or with the culture at large)?

- Share an example of a time when you have witnessed love be an overwhelming demonstration of Jesus to a skeptical unbeliever.

■ Going Forward

Break into pairs and discuss these next two questions:

- Describe someone you admire for his/her ability to share his or her faith. How does she talk about her faith? How does he demonstrate God's love to others? Share some examples.

- In what ways do you want to be more like that person? Be specific.

Gather back together as a group and read this quote:

If the gospel isn't good news for everybody, then it isn't good news for anybody. And this is because the most powerful things happen when the church surrenders its desire to convert people and to convince them to join. It is when the church gives itself away in radical acts of service and compassion, expecting nothing in return, that the way of Jesus is most vividly put on display. To do this, the church must stop thinking about everybody primarily in categories of in or out, saved or not, believer or nonbeliever. Besides the fact that these terms are offensive to those who are the "un" and "non," they work against Jesus's teachings about how we are to treat each other. Jesus commanded us to love our neighbor, and our neighbor can be anybody. —Rob Bell in *Velvet Elvis*

- Do you agree or disagree with Bell's statement? Why? Share which words or phrases stand out to you most and why.

Take turns sharing the name of one skeptical friend, family member, or acquaintance with whom you desire to share your faith. Write down the names everyone in the group shares, then take time to pray for each of those people, asking God to draw them to himself.

Commit to pray through the list each day during the next week.

■ Want to Explore More?

Recommended Resources

How to Talk About Jesus Without Freaking Out: An Easy-to-Use Practical Guide to Relationship Witnessing, Jim & Karen Covell, Victoria Michaels Rogers (Multnomah Publishers, 2000; ISBN 1576737373)

Know Why You Believe, Paul E. Little (InterVarsity Press, 2000; ISBN 083082250X)

Letters from a Skeptic: A Son Wrestles with His Father's Questions about Christianity, Dr. Gregory A. Boyd and Edward K. Boyd (Cook Communications, 1994; ISBN 1564762440)

The New Evidence that Demands a Verdict, Josh McDowell (Thomas Nelson Publishers, 1999; ISBN 0785242198)

Outflow: Outward-Focused Living in a Self-Focused World, Dave Ping and Steve Sjogren (Group Publishing, 2006; ISBN 9780764434044)

Permission Evangelism: When to Talk, When to Walk, Michael L. Simpson (David C. Cook, 2003; ISBN 0781439086)

Velvet Elvis: Repainting the Christian Faith, Rob Bell (Zondervan, 2005; ISBN 031026345X)

What does nerdy Ned

Flanders tell us about the

pros and cons of seeking to

be culturally relevant?

SCRIPTURE FOCUS

John 15:1–16:4

1 Corinthians 9:19–23

IS CULTURAL RELEVANCE IRRELEVANT?

■

The Simpsons's Ned Flanders is a model Christian citizen who seeks to live a holy and godly life and love his neighbor sacrificially. But instead of leading people to Jesus, Flanders's nerdiness and holy living turns his neighbors off to his message. He's derided as a "Charlie Church" and "God Boy," and his next-door neighbor, Homer Simpson, calls him "a big, four-eyed lame-o." Is this how non-Christians view us? If so, why? And is nerdiness a stumbling block to the gospel, or is being un-hip simply the side effect of following Jesus? Looming large above these issues is an even broader question: *Should* Christians seek to be culturally relevant? Is cultural relevance a worthy goal or just a huge distraction from more important pursuits? We'll explore these important issues as we examine Mark I. Pinsky's article "From Davey & Goliath to Homer and Ned" and Andy Crouch's article "The End of Relevance."

■ Before You Meet

Read "From *Davey & Goliath* to Homer and Ned" by Mark I. Pinsky from *Christianity Today* magazine and "The End of Relevance" by Andy Crouch from *re:generation Quarterly*.

FROM *DAVEY & GOLIATH* TO HOMER AND NED

Steve Tompkins believes God has a sense of humor.

By Mark I. Pinsky

Steve Tompkins, a veteran of three seasons with *The Simpsons* during the mid-1990s, is one of the most distinctive voices for values in Hollywood, but he is wary of being identified as a Christian, in part because the label can be the kiss of death for a comedy writer. "The two are seen as antithetical," he says, perplexed by the notion that a self-described class clown should have to choose between the kingdom of heaven and a successful writing career. "I do believe that Jesus is the Son of God, that he was crucified and that he rose again."

Tompkins grew up Episcopalian in an upscale Massachusetts town, attending the same church as the novelist John Updike. He remembers a childhood of watching *Davey & Goliath*, an early animated show produced by Lutherans, before leaving for church on Sunday mornings. Tompkins drifted from faith in his twenties. Then he had what he calls a "reconversion experience" while writing for *The Simpsons*, though he emphasizes it was unrelated to his work.

Tompkins showed clips from *Simpsons* episodes when he spoke as part of Fuller Theological Seminary's Reel Spirituality series last fall. His topic: "Does God Have a Sense of Humor?" Writing for Homer, Marge, Bart, and Lisa was a challenge. "There were some rabid atheists at *The Simpsons*," he says, but "no matter how twisted the story, no matter how profane the jokes, goodness wins, goodness prevails. No matter how much those writers pride themselves as being atheists, probably deep down they're not.

"At *The Simpsons* you are reined in," he says. "You can't stick your neck out and do anything that's overtly religious on its face. You must undercut it. There's a gag reflex in comedy writers to undercut any honest religious sentiment. It is easier to pass a camel through the eye of a needle than it is to make a comedy writer quote Scripture with a straight face."

The key, he says, is "respecting the faith of the characters because it's true to the characters. I think that's what's going on in the best moments of *The Simpsons*. . . . Marge's faith is respected because that is a huge part of who she is as a character. Homer has no faith, so we use him to tromp over Marge's faith, or whatever needs to be done comedically."

Tompkins worked on several *Simpsons* episodes that dealt with Christian faith, including "Hurricane Neddy," in which Ned has his faith tested in Job-inspired proportions. "There is a tremendous amount of affection for Ned" among the writers, he says.

Tompkins says he is a mostly secular writer. "I had no ax to grind at *The Simpsons*," he says. "I believe the quality of humor is in indirect proportion to one's true belief. . . . The more those beliefs are put in, the less funny it gets."

These days, Tompkins' greatest source of pride is *The PJs*, a prime-time Sunday show on the WB Network that he created with comedian Eddie Murphy. Tompkins says that including a spiritual dimension on *The PJs* presents a different challenge than on *The Simpsons*. *The PJs* focuses on the life of Thurgood Stubbs, an African American who works as a building superintendent in an inner-city housing project.

Last year Tompkins shepherded to the screen what he calls "the most manifestly Christian episode that has aired in television history." It was inspired by a screening of Robert Duvall's feature film, *The Apostle*, at an earlier event in the Reel Spirituality series. What the comedy writer had in mind for Thurgood, a rough-edged, occasionally profane man, was nothing less than a direct encounter with the divine, one in which "the character had faith and never questioned it."

Thurgood's encounter with God "wasn't a mistake," Tompkins says. "It was not a delusion from mixing Clorox bleach and ammonia. . . . I was going to give him a real conversion experience—born again. I didn't try to second-guess it or minimize it or undercut it. He saw God. He did not ask himself, 'Am I going crazy?' What he said was, 'I saw God. Now what do I do with it?'"

Mark I. Pinsky is a senior reporter who covers religion for The Orlando Sentinel.

("From Davey & Goliath to Homer and Ned" was first published in *Christianity Today*, 2001)

THE END OF RELEVANCE

By Andy Crouch

(This article was written in part as a response to the events of September 11, 2001.)

Farewell, Generations X and Y. Adios, Millennials. Ma'a salâma, postmodernity.
Algebraic symbols of the unknown, feeble attempts to draw meaning from the turning of a few zeros on the Western odometer, epochal placeholders, your usefulness—already fading long before 11 September—is past. We are no longer, as Richard John Neuhaus put it so trenchantly this week, "on a hedonistic holiday from history." History is back. And we're all in it together.

If there is one lesson the church can learn from 11 September, it's the futility of trying to be relevant to the culture. How many PowerPoint presentations on the characteristics of—take your pick—"postmodern culture," of "young people today," of "what seekers are looking for" are going to be dragged to the Trash icon in the next few months? The ill-fated attempt to move from *description* of culture to *prediction* always eventually founders on the sheer contingency of human life, the refusal of history to be anything but a random walk. From the length of hemlines to the list of things that "everybody knows," culture always zags when the experts think it will zig.

It's happened thousands of times before—from the Babylonian juggernaut rolling into Jerusalem in 587 BCE to the five-week roll of the dice that gave us our current president. On 11 September, it happened again.

Shortly before an airplane crashed into the Pentagon a few miles from where I sat toying with the remains of an oversized banana muffin, I had said to a colleague with a perfectly straight face, "Like most people my age, I have very few real heroes." Oh, I was a Gen Xer straight out of central casting—quick to see the flawed human core of every noble endeavor, emphatically including my own.

Well, forget it. I have hundreds of heroes now. Every fire fighter who was going up the stairs of the World Trade Center when the occupants were going down. The passengers on United 93 who fought for the privilege of choosing exactly where they would be smashed into oblivion. Jeremy Glick, age 31, who called his wife from that flight and told her, she said, "'I love you,' a thousand times, over and over and over again." Our president and the team around him who have the terrifying responsibility of leadership in this moment and who, fragile and inadequate as they must feel, are stepping up to that challenge.

These stories and thousands more—tragic, terrible, and triumphant alike—have demolished so many fantasies that occupied us a few days ago. Britney Spears's appearance at the MTV Music Awards, and her decision that, since she already appeared all but naked in last year's show, she might as well add a live snake to the act this time, now seems worse than a bad joke. It is not insignificant that the entertainment industry, professional sports, even *Disney World*, for goodness sake—in short, all our usual means of averting that quintessentially American horror, boredom—came to a halt. Long ago having decided to ignore such things, I have no idea what hot new fashion trend suburban girls were coveting in the malls of America on Monday afternoon. Now, I bet, neither do they.

It is so easy now to see that trying to be "relevant to the culture"— the culture of the upticking (though temporarily depressed) NASDAQ, the culture of freedom *from* with no countervailing freedom *for*, the culture of endless preoccupation with (and profit from) the tiniest differences in taste, the culture of extended adolescence, the culture of must-have $150 sneakers, the culture of extreme-sports adrenaline and scar-as-fashion-accessory, the culture of whatever latest band the slightly desperate marketeers thought would make a good cover for *Rolling Stone*, the culture of going to a "good" college and living in a "good" neighborhood and raising "good" kids while holding down a "good" job (at someplace like the World Trade Center, perhaps?)—that trying to be relevant to that culture was tantamount to tending bar in the Far City while the Prodigal Son's wallet was still bulging with banknotes. Like some pathologically insecure character in a sitcom, churches have done everything but, well, dance naked with a snake to try to get the attention of America's sons and daughters while they, happily running up the bills on mom and dad's credit cards, enjoyed all the fun that money could buy.

The result is a surfeit of evangelical Christians who, assuming that the *gospel* side of the eternal dance between gospel and culture is pretty much figured out, have devoted themselves to figuring out how to get the attention of the *culture*. It's the same project that occupied post-war mainline Protestantism, and it threatens to have the same result—a hollowed-out gospel (back then, it was "the fatherhood of God and the brotherhood of man") being proffered to a culture that ever so quickly moves on to the next new thing. We have become experts at exegeting the culture, and novices at exegeting the gospel. But our endless explorations of the nuances of postmodern, Generation-Fill-In-the-Blank culture now have as much relevance as last Tuesday morning's *Wall Street Journal*.

At moments like this certain segments of the church start predicting "revival." It probably won't be that simple, or that easy. For these are neither simple nor easy times—if for no other reason than the fact that unless the coming revival brings millions to faith in Allah the Most Merciful and Muhammad his Messenger, the next wave of terrorists is not likely to give a damn.

What is needed in this moment is nothing less than virtue—which is to revival what Thanksgiving dinner is to McDonald's. There are questions of societal virtue (notwithstanding Reinhold Niebuhr's caution about "immoral society"). What does it mean to be prudent in the pursuit of justice? Where is the line between force and violence? What does it mean to be *safe?* What does it mean to be *free?* What does it mean for the United States—still the most powerful country in the world—to serve the poor and oppressed (such as the people of Afghanistan) even while it pursues its enemies?

And there are questions of personal virtue. When a bomb goes off next door to our home, which way will we run? What do we truly hope for, in this life and the next? Do our lives reflect even slightly the convictions we claim to hold?

The answers to all of these questions depend not one bit upon an understanding of last month's top hip-hop artists. They hang entirely upon how deeply and richly we have read the Word of God—that endlessly fascinating tragicomic love story—and how deeply and richly we have known the Word made flesh—that incomparably human one, the Son of Man, who discloses to us, and creates in us, the life that is really life. These answers come only through a sustained collective listening to a Word that cannot be distilled into sound bites or six easy steps. They come at the painful price of self-renunciation, humility, patience, and discipline. They come finally not as answers at all but as possibilities, ways of living differently, "as dying, and see—we are alive; as punished, and yet not killed; as sorrowful, yet always rejoicing; as poor, yet making many rich; as having nothing, and yet possessing everything."

Who we are, and who we become, in this moment will disclose whether turn-of-the-millennium American Christianity was made of gold or straw. Because a desperately searching world doesn't care how hip you are. They want to know which way you were going on the stairs.

Andy Crouch is the editor of the Christian Vision Project and served as editor-in-chief of re:generation quarterly.

("The End of Relevance" was first published in *re:generation Quarterly*, Spring 2003.)

For more insightful articles from *Christianity Today* magazine and its sister publications, visit http://www.ctlibrary.com/ and subscribe now.

■ Open Up

Select one of these activities to launch your discussion time.

Option 1

Discuss one of these icebreaker questions:

• Think back to your years in high school. Would you characterize your-self as a nerdy dork, as cool and hip, or somewhere in between? Why? Looking back, what are some of the most embarrassing things about the way you dressed, spoke, or the things you liked to do at that age?

• Now think about the here and now: Have you ever been embarrassed by the nerdiness, squareness, or insularity of fellow Christians? When?

Option 2

Watch a short scene from *The Simpsons* TV show or movie featuring Ned Flanders. (See the list of recommended episodes on p.75). Then talk about these questions together:

- For many, Ned Flanders embodies the cultural stereotypes about evangelical Christians. What are some of the stereotypes of Christians you observed in the clip?

- What about Ned Flanders attracts you? What repels you? How might you see Flanders differently if you were not a Christian?

■ The Issue

When many Americans think of the words *evangelical* and *Christian*, the person that comes to mind, even before Billy Graham, is animated sitcom character Ned Flanders from *The Simpsons*. "The mustache, thick glasses, green sweater, and irrepressibly cheerful demeanor of Ned Flanders, Homer Simpson's next-door neighbor, have made him an indelible figure, the evangelical known most intimately to nonevangelicals," writes *Orlando Sentinel* religion reporter Mark I. Pinsky, author of *The Gospel According to The Simpsons*.

Fortunately, Flanders doesn't fit common stereotypes of conservative Christians in popular culture. He isn't a modern-day Elmer Gantry, scheming to use religion to advance his own interests. Nor is he a hypocrite, crusading against the moral failures of his neighbors while ignoring the logs in his own eye. He is an introspective, honest Christian who tries desperately to love his neighbor to the utmost, regularly putting others' lives before his own.

CURRENT ISSUES: ENGAGING THE CULTURE

And yet people in the town of Springfield don't aspire to be like Flanders—and neither do people in the real world. That's because he is seen (in Homer Simpson's words) as a nerd, a square, "a big, four-eyed lame-o." Is his nerdiness a stumbling block for evangelism? Is it a part of his personality, or a natural outcome of trying to live a godly life? Is Christianity inevitably un-hip?

- Do you think churches and individual Christians should try to be "hip" or "cool" in order to appeal to nonbelievers? Why or why not?

In his article, Andy Crouch described some Christian efforts to be culturally relevant this way: "Like some pathologically insecure character in a sitcom, churches have done everything but, well, dance naked with a snake to try to get the attention of America's sons and daughters."

- Do you think there is a danger in Christian efforts to be culturally relevant? When have you observed examples of Christian efforts to be relevant going too far?

■ Reflect

Take a moment to read John 15:1–16:4 and 1 Corinthians 9:19–23 on your own. Jot down a few notes and observations about these passages: What themes and ideas seem most important? What similarities or differences do you see between these passages? What questions do these passages bring up?

■ Let's Explore

Ultimately, as follower of Jesus we will always be alienated from "the world."

- It's common for Christians to believe that if they live holy enough lives, or if they are joyful enough, or if they seek God hard enough, then others will naturally be attracted to them—and thus, to their faith. Is this a realistic expectation? When have you experienced this to be true in your own life? Or, alternately, do your experiences with non-Christians lead you to a different conclusion? Explain.

Read John 15:1–16:4. After encouraging his disciples with words of love, calling them friends, and comparing their relationship to a vine and its branches, Jesus darkly warns that this relationship will mean hatred by the world and persecution, even death.

- What does Jesus mean by "the world"? What other verses come to mind that focus on "the world"? How might they illuminate Jesus's meaning here?

Commentator Rodney Whitacre writes, "The world's hatred . . . is an encouragement to the disciples since it is due to the difference Jesus has made within them. This does not mean the world has no hatred for others besides Christians. Nor does it mean that someone who is hated by the world is necessarily being true to God. But Jesus does say that those who are his disciples are quite distinct from all that is in rebellion against God and should not be surprised when opposition arises" (*IVP New Testament Commentary IV: John*, 1999).

- How can we tell when the world's hatred is because of obedience to Christ rather than something else?

- Are the Neds you know (both on TV and in real life) disliked, even hated, because they're "goody goodies" who are trying to live holy lives or because of other reasons?

- When have you felt like an outsider—or even disliked or hated—because of your faith?

Becoming "all things to all men" is a call to sacrifice.

- Wanting to fit in is a natural social desire for most people. How much does the need to be admired and respected (even loved) by others affect your faith and life? In what ways?

Read 1 Corinthians 9:19–23. Jesus's warning that we will be hated by the world does not give us an excuse to completely isolate ourselves from it. Indeed, we are called to "go into all the world," and to be "the light of the world." Paul tells how he did this by becoming "all things to all men so that by all possible means I might save some." But what does this mean? Is Paul suggesting that he used deception or trickery in evangelism?

Several early church writers wrestled with this question and concluded that Paul was not deceptive for the sake of the gospel, but rather was empathetic. One scholar (later called Ambrosiaster, though that was not his name), writing between 366 and 384, wrote, "Did Paul merely pretend to be all things to all men, in the way that flatterers do? No. He was a man of God and a doctor of the spirit who could diagnose every pain, and with great diligence he tended them and sympathized with them all. We all have something or other in common with everyone. This empathy is what Paul embodied in dealing with each particular person."

Augustine agreed. "Paul was not pretending to be what he is not but showing compassion," he wrote. "A person who nurses a sick man becomes, in a sense, sick himself, not by pretending to have a fever but by thinking sympathetically how he would like to be treated if he were sick himself" (*Ancient Christian Commentary on Scripture: New Testament Vol. VII, IVP*, 1999).

- Note that Paul begins this section by saying that he makes himself a slave, giving up certain rights. How is a sacrificial act of "becoming all things to all men" different from a non-sacrificial act of just trying to fit in?

- If Paul had written, "To the hip I became hip, and to the square I became square," what might this look like? Would Paul have written this at all?

- If Ned were a real person trying to win more people to Jesus, do you think he should make a conscious effort to "make himself a slave" to fashion? To be less upbeat? Are there aspects of his personality he should change? Why or why not?

■ Going Forward

In a *Christianity Today* interview, Eugene Peterson questioned the pursuit of cultural relevance, saying:

> When you start tailoring the gospel to the culture, whether it's a youth culture, a generation culture or any other kind of culture, you have taken the guts out of the gospel. The gospel of Jesus Christ is not the kingdom of this world. It's a different kingdom. . . . I think relevance is a crock. I don't think people care a whole lot about what kind of music you have or how you shape the service. They want a place where God is taken seriously, where they're taken seriously, where there is no manipulation of their emotions or their consumer needs. ("Spirituality for All the Wrong Reasons," March 2005)

Andy Crouch wrote in his article that "a desperately searching world doesn't care how hip you are. They want to know which way you were going on the stairs."

- What's your response to Peterson and Crouch? Do you think cultural relevance should play a part in evangelism? Why or why not?

- What does it mean to you to be relevant as a Christian?

• Do you ever worry that being more open about your faith will cause others to think of you as odd, annoying, or nerdy? How do you desire to be more bold in living out your faith in the world?

Take turns sharing one specific sphere of your life in which you feel God challenging you to be more purposeful and open in sharing the gospel through words and actions (such as your workplace, a particular social group, or a specific relationship). Write down what everyone in the group shares, then take time to pray for each person in your group, asking God to embolden each of you.

Commit to pray for your group members over the next week.

■ Want to Explore More?

Recommended Resources

The Simpsons Archive (www.snpp.com). See especially "The Ned Flandiddly-anders File" (www.snpp.com/guides/flanders.file.html) and "Religion on the Simpsons" (www.snpp.com/guides/religion.html)

The Gospel According to The Simpsons, Mark I. Pinsky (Westminster John Knox Press, 2001; ISBN 0664224199)

The Gospel According to the Simpsons: Leaders Guide for Group Study, Mark I. Pinsky and Samuel F. (Skip) Parvin (Westminster John Knox Press, 2006; ISBN 066422590X)

"Ned Flanders, My Hero," Frederica Mathewes-Green, Beliefnet (http://www.beliefnet.com/story/10/story_1052.html)

"How Ned Flanders Became a Role Model," Giles Wilson, BBC (http://news.bbc.co.uk/2/hi/uk/2175870.stm)

The Simpsons DVDs available from Fox Home Entertainment.

The following episodes are based around Ned Flanders:

- 7F08 (Season two): "Dead Putting Society"
- 7F23 (Season three): "When Flanders Failed"
- 1F14 (Season five): "Homer Loves Flanders"
- 1F18 (Season five): "Sweet Seymour Skinner's Bad— Song"
- 1F22 (Season six): "Bart of Darkness"
- 3F01 (Season seven): "Home Sweet Home-Diddly-Dum-Doodily"
- 4F07 (Season eight): "Hurricane Neddy"
- 4F18 (Season eight): "In Marge We Trust"
- 5F06 (Season nine): "Realty Bites"
- AABF06 (Season ten): "Viva Ned Flanders"
- BABF10 (Season eleven): "Alone Again, Natura-Diddly"
- CABF15 (Season twelve): "I'm Goin' To Praiseland"
- EABF08 (Season fourteen): "A Star is Born-Again"
- EABF13 (Season fourteen): "Dude, Where's My Ranch?"
- GABF02 (Season sixteen): "Homer and Ned's Hail Mary Pass"
- GABF15 (Season sixteen): "Home Away from Homer"

What are the key

differences between trendy,

pop culture "spirituality"

and authentic, distinctly

Christian spirituality?

SCRIPTURE FOCUS

Ezekiel 8:1–18

Romans 7:18–8:16, 8:26–27

A SPIRITUALITY
SMORGASBORD

■

Pop culture gurus abound to guide us in all aspects of
our lives: what to eat, what to wear, even how to fold our
dinner napkins. This influence of celebrity on cultural
trends is certainly nothing new; but perhaps what is new,
at least in the past decade or so, is the profound influence
celebrities are beginning to have in the arena of spirituality.
Messages abound, hyping self-esteem to a religious level
or encouraging us to experience our "higher power" in any
form he or she chooses. And perhaps no cultural icon is
more well-known for her effect on American spirituality
than the queen of day-time talk: Oprah Winfrey.

The feel-good, postmodern spirituality espoused by
Oprah and many others is all about self-fulfillment . . .
but is it really so fulfilling? Why are so many people
buying into it? Why are even many *Christians* buying
into it? Using two *Christianity Today* articles,
"The Church of O" and "It's Not About Us," this
study will cut through the fluff of popular

"spirituality" and explore what the Bible says about authentic Christian spirituality.

■ Before You Meet

Read "The Church of O" by LaTonya Taylor and "It's Not About Us" by Edith M. Humphrey from *Christianity Today* magazine.

THE CHURCH OF O

With a congregation of 22 million viewers, Oprah Winfrey has become one of the most influential spiritual leaders in America.

By LaTonya Taylor

"When you lose a loved one, you gain an angel whose name you know," said Oprah Winfrey to the thousands of mourners gathered in Yankee Stadium just 12 days after 9/11. "Over 6,000, and counting, angels added to the spiritual roster these past two weeks. It is my prayer that they will keep us in their sight with a direct line to our hearts." After reminding mourners that "hope lives, prayer lives, love lives," she offered an affirmation tinged with challenge and benediction: "May we all leave this place and not let one single life have passed in vain. May we leave this place determined to now use every moment that we yet live to turn up the volume in our own lives, to create deeper meaning, to know what really matters."

Fast forward to Chicago a few weeks later. About three hundred people are seated around a small wooden platform at Harpo Studios for a taping of "The Oprah Show." After the show, as is her custom, Oprah entertains questions from curious audience members. What, one woman asks, is one of the most important experiences she's ever had? A common question, but Oprah obliges her and refers to the infamous 1998 trial in which a group of Texas cattlemen sued her after she expressed reluctance to eat burgers ever again during a show on mad cow disease. The cattlemen's lawyer had accused her of intentionally causing beef stock prices to fall.

She won the trial, Oprah told the audience, when she began to see it as a metaphor for life's trials. "I kept asking God, 'What is the deeper meaning of this? It can't be about burgers,'" she said. Then she received the revelation: "I became calm inside myself and I thought, The outside world is always going to be telling you one thing, have one impression—accusatory, blaming, and so forth. And you are to stand still inside yourself and know the truth, and let it set you free. And in that moment, I won that trial."

As the story reaches its climax, a small, elderly black woman in a turquoise Sunday suit rises from her seat and claps her hands. "Yes!" she shouts with the joy of one who likes a good testimony. The audience claps approvingly.

These two incidents—the New York memorial service and Oprah's informal testimony time with her studio audience—illustrate the blurring of the popular and pastoral, the self-help and the sacred, in the woman who is Oprah.

Since 1994, when she abandoned traditional talk-show fare for more edifying content, and 1998, when she began "Change Your Life TV," Oprah's most significant role has become that of spiritual leader. To her audience of more than 22 million mostly female viewers, she has become a postmodern priestess—an icon of church-free spirituality.

"Oprah Winfrey arguably has more influence on the culture than any university president, politician, or religious leader, except perhaps the Pope," noted a 1994 *Vanity Fair* article. Indeed, much like a healthy church, Oprah creates community, provides information, and encourages people to evaluate and improve their lives.

Oprah's brand of spirituality cannot simply be dismissed as superficial civil religion or so much New Age psychobabble, either. It goes much deeper. The story of her personal journey to worldwide prominence could be viewed as a window into American spirituality at the beginning of the 21st century—and into the challenges it poses for the church.

Becoming 'Oprah'

From the beginning, Oprah regularly featured spiritual themes on her shows. But her emergence as a spiritual force in her own right began with the 1994–95 season. Oprah has said that each year she asks God for a different gift or insight. In 1994, she says, it was clarity. "I have become more clear about my purpose in television and this show," she told a reporter that year. She decided to clean up her program.

Whatever the reason for her shift in direction, Oprah has never looked back. She has successfully separated herself from the Jerry Springers of the world, not only through rejecting the My-Husband-Ain't-My-Baby's-Daddy content but also by methodically directing her audience to take an inward focus. For example, Oprah introduced the "Remembering Your Spirit" segment in 1998 as a way to challenge viewers to personally apply the lessons learned on each show. Oprah often refers to her show as "my ministry," and examples of her benevolence abound. She gives liberally of her time and money, convincing others to do the same through her Angel Network and the Use Your Life Award. She has funded scholarships at historically black colleges, rescued a local Special Olympics program, written checks to churches, and moved families out of the inner city. She is the national spokeswoman for A Better Chance, a program that gives disadvantaged students opportunities to attend top secondary schools. In 1991, Oprah promoted the National Child Protection Act, also known as the "Oprah Bill," which created a database to track child abusers. Bill Clinton signed the legislation in 1993.

Oprah clearly believes part of her role as a talk show host is to call her audience to some sort of higher plane. The theological nature of that higher plane and her methods for getting there are what sound alarms for many of her Christian critics.

What Does She Believe?

"I like Oprah," says preacher and Bible teacher Brenda Salter McNeil. "I'm a closet groupie, though, because her theology's a little off. But I think she has one of the most positive programs on television." McNeil, founder and president of Overflow Ministries in Chicago and a former regional director for InterVarsity Christian Fellowship, is one of many

Christians who admire Oprah as a communicator and humanitarian, but who have reservations about her spiritual beliefs. Oprah's public theology reflects a trend among some African Americans to compile a belief system from several philosophies, McNeil says. "There's a blending that's happening in the African-American community now of this kind of New Age, Afrocentric spirituality that has a measure of truth but never forces people into a clear relationship with Jesus Christ."

On a show broadcast last November, Oprah explored the value of spiritual beliefs in the wake of the September 11 tragedy. "Today, whatever it is you believe most deeply, now is the time to embrace it," she told her audience. "I say to people, if you have no faith at this time I don't know what to say to you. . . . If you don't know what you believe in when you're going through difficult times, then you feel shaky and unbalanced."

But what core beliefs is Oprah turning to now? There are no authorized biographies of Oprah Winfrey, and she declined CT's requests for an interview. Several principles emerge, however, from a close reading of her show, guests who speak on spiritual matters, and other interviews she has given.

Through her discussions with New Age author and thinker Gary Zukav, for instance, Oprah emphasizes that we are more than physical beings. "I believe that life is eternal," she has said. "I believe that it takes on other forms."

She told Zukav, "I am creation's daughter. I am more than my physical self. I am more than the job I do. I am more than the external definitions that I have given myself. . . . Those are all extensions of who I define myself to be, but ultimately I am Spirit come from the greatest Spirit. I am Spirit."

Through a succession of guests with eclectic religious ties, including Zukav, Carolyn Myss, Marianne Williamson, Iyanla Vanzant, and Deepak Chopra, Oprah's show has normalized a generic spirituality that perceives all religions as equally valid paths to God. The show also presents an á la carte blend of religious concepts, from karmic destiny (Zen Buddhism) to reincarnation (Hinduism).

"There's this assumption [in Oprah's spirituality] that whatever is really true can be found in many different paths," says Elliot Miller, author of *A Crash Course on the New Age Movement* (Baker, 1999) and editor in chief of *Christian Research Journal.* "Out of that, there is an effort to create a contemporary spirituality that is suitable to the postmodern temperament."

Miller, who taught a seminar at last year's Cornerstone Festival that analyzed Oprah's beliefs, calls her a representative of the new spirituality that defines postmodernism. "What we're dealing with is sort of amorphous," he says, "because it isn't some religion that is coming in and displacing Christianity. In fact, a lot of people who embrace the new spirituality would say they draw most heavily from the Christian tradition."

So where does Christ fit into the Oprah brand of spirituality? While Oprah herself makes few references to Jesus, if she shares the views of many of her guests, "she would believe that Jesus is like an ascended master, a God-realized teacher, someone who completely expressed God in their life," Miller says.

Consequently, Jesus Christ is not seen as a personal Savior or God incarnate but as a good teacher who shows us how to achieve what he has achieved. This view renders Christian distinctives such as salvation by grace, redemption through the Cross, the Trinity, and the Last Judgment irrelevant.

Still, it is clear that Oprah retains some elements of her Baptist upbringing. Her show has a "churchy" feel, the theme music has a gospel flair, and gospel artists such as Yolanda Adams, BeBe and CeCe Winans, Wintley Phipps, and Donnie McClurkin are occasional guests. Christian professionals such as Stephen Arterburn, author of several books on therapeutic issues, and relationship experts Les and Leslie Parrott have shared their expertise. In her *O: The Oprah Magazine* monthly column, "What I Know for Sure," Oprah refers frequently to the Bible, her church background, and lessons God has taught her. In earlier interviews, she has spoken about reading the Bible, praying, and meditating daily. She has also said that her faith has sustained her, and spoken of "the absolute responsibility to live our lives as a praise." A *People* magazine article about Oprah's Personal Growth Summit tour last summer noted that while she refers to a "higher power" on television, at a Raleigh, North Carolina, summit she spoke "with a preacher's confidence of 'the Creator,' 'the Lord,' even 'my blessed Savior.'"

Oprah's Christian heritage informs her show and magazine in more than cosmetic ways, some observers believe. "She has come to understand some deeply biblical principles about life," McNeil says. "In Proverbs it says, 'As a man (or a person) thinks in his heart, so is he.' I think that she and others have come to understand that we participate with God in creating reality. That we can limit ourselves by how we think, and we can also begin to expand our potential by how we think and what we believe."

The Seekers' Seeker

What does Oprah's appeal to so many Americans, particularly women, tell us about current American spirituality?

First, so-called secular Americans remain spiritually hungry. This may be because so much of our culture is secular. When someone like Oprah comes along and is open about spirituality, and in a winsome way, people are fascinated. Oprah's increased popularity when she became more publicly spiritual is just one evidence of this.

Second, Americans are interested in practical spirituality. "Oprah is concerned with helping us live better and more authentically," says Robert Johnston, professor of theology and culture at Fuller Theological Seminary in Pasadena, California. Brenda Salter McNeil adds: "People today are really looking for a message of salvation that literally has the power to change their lives. Oprah's greatest success is that she's living proof of what she believes."

Indeed, part of Oprah's appeal is that she motivates people to make practical, lasting changes in their lives. Whether she is speaking about diet and exercise, promoting a new book, or hosting the straight-talking Dr. Phil, her gospel is an empowering one: you can change.

Third, Americans yearn for a hopeful spirituality. During one broadcast, a viewer confides that she purchased a pair of Oprah's size-10 shoes at a charity sale and would stand in them, size 7 feet slid toward the front, whenever she felt powerless or small. As she learned more from the show, she said, she didn't need them as often. She has changed. The woman drops her head into her hands, and Oprah dabs at her eyes. Oprah's brand of spirituality encourages and inspires millions.

Fourth, many Americans like to dabble in a variety of belief systems. When the mother of missing congressional intern Chandra Levy told *The Washington Times* that she was a "Heinz 57 mutt" in her spirituality—drawing from Judaism, Christianity, Buddhism, and other religions—she verbalized a sentiment common to many in Oprah's audience. And Oprah herself has said, "One of the biggest mistakes humans make is to believe there is only one way. Actually, there are many diverse paths leading to what you call God."

None of this is new, of course. Social commentators have noted such American trends since Alexis de Toqueville's *Democracy in America* (1835). The Church of O merely brings this into focus in the 21st century.

What the Oprah phenomenon also shows, though, is that this brand of spirituality is ultimately unsatisfying. Perhaps the most telling thing about Oprah's role as a spiritual leader to the seeking masses is that she herself is such an ambitious seeker. Indeed, the smorgasbord of religions and ideas that make up her belief system suggest that she still has not found what she's looking for.

The question for Christians is this: What can we do to help Oprah and her disciples find what they are ultimately seeking—the power, grace, and love that can only be found through a personal relationship with Jesus Christ?

The answers are not obvious, but the need to find them is as urgent as ever.

LaTonya Taylor is the editorial resident at Christianity Today.

(This article is excerpted from "The Church of O," first published in *Christianity Today*, April 1, 2002 • Vol. 46, No. 4, Page 38.)

IT'S NOT ABOUT US

Modern spirituality begins and ends with the self; Christian spirituality, with the Alpha and the Omega.

By Edith M. Humphrey

I think I first noticed it six years ago. One of my daughters returned home from a school trip to Iowa and remarked that she would never again be embarrassed by our family's custom of giving thanks before meals.

She had been hosted by an academic family whose mother was also the minister of a novel spiritual community. Their family's time of meditation focused on the spiritual value of life-mediating crystals placed upon the mantelpiece over the fireplace.

"And I thought we were weird!" remarked my daughter, then eleven years old.

Attitudes toward the spiritual have changed considerably in the past few decades, away from a "scientific" dismissal of the nonmaterial toward an easy acceptance of all things mysterious.

Riding a New Wave

Spirituality is back in fashion. A sampling of spirituality Web sites to be found on Metacrawler, randomly selected: Spirituality for Today; Women's Spirituality Book List; The Spirited Walker: Fitness Walking for Clarity, Balance, and Spiritual Connection; Medical Intuition; Jesuit Spirituality; Native American Spirituality; Transgender Spirituality; Spirit Tools for a New Age (pyramids, wands, daggers, and pendulums—sounds like Harry Potter books!); Spirituality and Health; Spirituality and Living Longer; The Inner Self Magazine: Spirituality as Opposed to Religion; Spirituality in the Workplace; Sex and Spirituality: Frequently Asked Questions; Apply Spiritual Ideas in Practical Ways; Spirituality Book—the Invisible Path to Success; Psychotherapy and Spirituality; The Spiritual Walk of the Labyrinth; and, last but not least, Male Spirituality.

How might we expect Christians to respond to this smorgasbord? It is clear that some have joined the growing trend to forge one's own "spirituality" in an eclectic manner rather than being guided by the wisdom of the Christian tradition alone. This seems to be true even in the relatively "conservative" context of Canada, where almost ninety percent of Canadians typically consider themselves as affiliated with a particular denomination—although they may have little deep experience or knowledge of their own tradition (or even of the Christian faith). Many approach their spiritual journey as artisans working on a bricolage, or a religious version of the song, "Mambo Number Five"— a little bit of gospel language here, a little bit of Celtic wisdom there, a little bit of karma in the sun.

Perhaps that is too flippant. Certainly, Christians are not the only ones with insight into the human spirit, and different human traditions may have wisdom to offer. Yet, if they are to remain faithful to their tradition, Christians should be on guard against a simple drift into the contemporary consumer mindset—represented by Andrew Walker, who declares, "We are no longer swayed by one religion alone. Many kinds are for sale, and compete for our attention. We, the consumers, are completely free."

Defining the Ephemeral

But what, after, all is "spirituality"? Most assume that spirituality is fundamentally about us. In her *Walking a Sacred Path*, Lauren Artress typifies our emptiness in this subjective manner: "We lost our sense of connection to ourselves and to the vast mystery of Creation."

For Artress, spirituality is about regaining a sense of connection to ourselves and to the Creation. Perhaps that is involved, but what about our connection to the Spirit of Truth, the one to whom our spirits are called to respond? How can a truncated spirituality, intent mainly upon finding an inner connection, be said to represent the Christian mind?

Christians proclaim the good news that God himself has visited humankind, dramatically and decisively, in the one who is God-with-us, Jesus the Lord—dying our death, conquering it in the resurrection, and ascending to the Father in a manifestation of triumph and glory. As a result of these particular events, the Holy Spirit has also come to dwell intimately with God's people, working out the reconciliation that has already been accomplished in Christ.

Part of the mystery of the Incarnation is that God has assumed human nature, taking it up into himself so that it may be both healed and glorified: body and soul, we have been visited by our Creator, and we see the location of this mystery in Jesus himself. Our spirit, will, heart, mind, passions, and body (which tend to war against each other), our interpersonal relationships, our relationship with the other parts of creation—all are out of joint. They all find their healing because of the initiative of God.

Further, because human nature has been taken up into God the Son, a new potential for intimate fellowship with God, and the glory that accompanies this, has now been forged.

The Link Made Possible

Adam and Eve walked with God. Fallen humanity, its spirit wounded, lost that ease of communion. Redeemed humanity has been sent the enlivening Spirit, who is himself a promise of the unimaginable intimacy to come when "we shall be like him, for we will see him as he is."

Paul looked forward to the final resurrection, when our very bodies, healed and new, will be completely animated or empowered by the "Spirit" rather than simply by "soul" as they now are (1 Cor. 15:42–49). He explains that while Adam was a "living soul," Jesus Christ, through the resurrection, has provided us with a "life-giving Spirit."

Notice that this is not an optimism born of confidence in the inner capacity of the human spirit, although Paul is well aware of the wonders held within the very good human creation of God. Rather, all this begins with the act of God, continues through the wooing of God's Spirit, and issues in the willing submission (there's an uncomfortable word) of the human spirit to him.

Here, then, are the two challenges that a Christian mind brings to the sometime inchoate and frequently narcissistic spiritualities of today: First, we can understand our human spirituality only in the light of our creatureliness—a fallen creatureliness at that—and that of God's initiative on our behalf.

Second, when we speak of our human spirit being linked to the divine Spirit, that can only make sense in the light of the particular one whose life, death, resurrection, and ascension have made that possible.

Christians know of one mediator, Jesus Christ, and of the particular, Holy Spirit of God, who is radically free to visit whom he chooses, whose role is to glorify and interpret Jesus to us, and who is not to be identified with a vague world-force or abstract power to be manipulated by us.

These two Christian challenges, our needy creaturely status, and the particularity of God's Spirit, over against other concepts of divinity, freedom or power, must stand. Yet they are not to be confused with a low view of humanity, or a triumphalism that declares that God's Spirit is only active among those who call themselves Christians.

What is to be affirmed is a sober but full assessment of the human condition and the human nature, alongside a joyful response to the particularity of God's clearest word, and most surprising revelation to humankind, his glory in the face of Jesus.

Experience It

Let's finish with some idea of what we might expect of a "Christian spirituality." Spirituality is the study (or better yet, the practice) of when or where or how the very Spirit of God meets with our spirits, both personally and corporately as the body of Christ. Yet, immediately in saying that, we know it to be skewed. For we have made the great Initiator, the Alpha, the object of our study; or we have turned our attention away from him to an experience.

Better, I think, for us to take seriously the saying, "A theologian is one who prays," and to take as our symbol of Christian spirituality the figure of the woman praying in the catacombs: she gazes toward heaven, her open hands raised with palms upward, aware of the human need, a powerful picture of the soul at prayer, or the church at prayer, or both together at prayer.

With her open hands she says to the Spirit, "Come!" Yet, in doing this, we only invite him to fill what is already his, for in him we live and move and have our being. Moreover, he himself is the gift of God's people together.

A full-bodied Christian spirituality, then, will lead us at every moment to invite God's Spirit to make a personal dwelling in our lives, knowing that we do this together, as the faithful in Christ. Inner and constant receptivity becomes an extension of our baptism, and an ongoing fulfillment of that unity that we experience and express around the Lord's Table.

As we enter into this adventure of communion with the one to whom we owe our very breath, meditation upon the Scriptures—the reading, marking, and inward digestion of them—is essential. Spirituality is not a private thing apart from what we have learned in Scripture but intimately connected with that story, those words, those pictures of the one we love. Spirituality begins with learning from him, not with human resolve for the esoteric, nor with a search for personal empowerment, nor with confidence in human solidarity.

It is at times of watching and in quietness—in our sober recognition that God is the Word and that our role is to attend—that our Lord comes to us. The human spirit hears the divine Spirit lovingly but powerfully encouraging us to live with him in the present, despite nostalgia for our past and fears or hopes for our future.

As C. S. Lewis puts it, we are called to attend to "eternity itself, and to that point of time which [we] call the present. For the present is the point at which time touches eternity. Of the present moment, and of it only, humans have an experience which God has of reality as a whole; in it alone freedom and actuality are offered to us."

Today is the time of salvation. In learning attentiveness toward him now, in putting aside all the distractions, memories, fears, and keen anticipations that crowd our minds, we become more fully what we are meant to be. We are on the way to becoming "prayer" before God, allowing his Spirit to pray within us where we are too weak or too simple to know how to pray.

In this way, we do not lose attentiveness toward the world, and toward others, paralyzed in a spiritual disconnection. Strangely, in seeking him, or rather in being sought, we find ourselves at home in the world in a new way, yearning and working for its renewal, which will be fulfilled when the time is ripe.

Part of our attentiveness today must surely mean that we take note of the new openness toward those things that could be considered "spiritual." Love will also dictate that in a well-meaning desire to build bridges we do not accept everything called "spiritual" and do not acquiesce to the malformed, underdeveloped, or human-centered approaches to "spirituality" we see everywhere.

Rather, may it be that we ourselves "acquire peace, and a multitude will be saved" (Seraphim of Sarov) as we live, speak, refrain from speaking, act, and pray in such a manner that the very Spirit of God is seen pointing toward the One who has loved us.

When we have the mind of Christ, the world itself, and especially every human person in it, becomes a window to us of his presence, his love, his peace, his power. In the words of Ephrem the Syrian, "Wherever we turn our eyes, there is God's symbol."

Christian spirituality is becoming present to the Lord, as he is always present to us. "Lord Jesus Christ, have mercy upon us sinners, your very own, and upon the whole world that you have made and have come to renew."

Edith M. Humphrey is professor of Scripture at Augustine College, Ottawa. This essay is adapted from a talk originally given at St. Paul University, Ottawa, in a session bringing together supporters of Augustine College, Redeemer College, and St. Paul University. An abbreviated version has appeared in the Dallas Morning News.

(This article is excerpted from "It's Not About Us," first published in *Christianity Today*, April 2, 2001, Vol. 45, No. 5, Page 66.)

For more insightful articles from *Christianity Today* magazine, visit http://www.ctlibrary.com/ and subscribe now.

■ Open Up

Select one of these activities to launch your discussion time.

Option 1

Discuss one of these icebreaker questions:

- Name a celebrity who is hero to you. Why do you admire that person?

- Oprah is just one of many celebrities (authors, musicians, movie stars) whose spiritual beliefs are admired and celebrated in popular culture. Who are some other celebrities that influence the way people view spirituality or religious experience? What is their message?

Option 2

Cut slips of paper so that there's one per group member. Write "T" on about one-third of the slips and "F" on the remaining slips. Fold up the slips, then pass them out. Each group member should keep the contents of his or her slip a secret.

Now take turns telling a short "fact" about your life—such as something you did as a child, a food you enjoy, or an odd experience you had. Here's the kicker: Those whose slip read "T" must say something that is *true*. Those whose slip said "F" must make up something *fictional*, but tell it as if it is true.

After you've each share something about yourself, work together to try to guess whose statements were true and whose were fictional.

Afterward, discuss these questions:

- What factors made you believe what others said? How did they persuade or influence you?

• When it comes to one's views on religion or spirituality, what factors do you think make celebrities' beliefs and ideas so convincing for others? Why do they hold so much sway in our culture?

■ The Issue

• People crave spiritual fulfillment. It's part of our nature. Describe a time when you had a meaningful "spiritual experience." What was it like?

• The term "spirituality" is widely used today. What, generally, do people mean by it? Would the spiritual experience you just described fit under the cultural definition of spirituality? Why or why not?

■ Reflect

Take a moment to read Ezekiel 8:1–18 and Romans 7:18–8:16, 8:26–27 on your own. Jot down a few notes and observations about the passages: What strong emotions, visual imagery, or metaphoric language in these passages stand out to you? What do you see as the key themes of each passage? What questions do these passages raise for you?

■ Let's Explore

We must reject the syncretism of "cafeteria-style" spirituality.

Though Oprah, like many celebrities, at times appears to cherish her Christian background and often promotes ideas that line up with biblical values, she's also made extremely unbiblical statements, such as this: "One of the biggest mistakes humans can make is to believe there is only one way. Actually, there are many diverse paths leading to what you call God."

Writer Elliot Miller sees the plurality in Oprah's belief system as representative of postmodern spirituality in general. "What we're dealing with is sort of amorphous," he says, "because it isn't some religion that is coming in and displacing Christianity. In fact, a lot of people who embrace the new spirituality would say they draw most heavily from the Christian tradition."

- How have you seen examples of this? When have you observed people adding ideas from non-Christian spirituality to their belief systems while still holding onto some aspects of traditional Christianity? Why do you think people do this?

In the Old Testament, the law expressly forbids the worshiping of any gods but Yahweh. God repeatedly admonishes Israel to keep the detestable practices of pagan nations from infiltrating their own worship ceremonies. This marriage of Yahweh worship with idolatry is called *syncretism*.

With the emergence of spiritual philosophies that encourage the cafeteria-style selection of beliefs and practices, syncretism is again a threat to the unadulterated worship of the Almighty God. Humphrey quotes one observer: "We are no longer swayed by one religion alone. Many kinds are for sale, and compete for our attention. We, the consumers, are completely free." How are Christians to respond to this smorgasbord? Read one example of God's response to syncretism in Ezekiel 8:1–18.

- What strong words and phrases does God use here? Why do you think he is so harsh?

- Do you think Christians can safely incorporate some aspects of modern spirituality into their lives without it being syncretistic? If so, which parts of modern spirituality do you feel are harmless? If not, why not?

Spiritual fulfillment comes not from a deeper connection with ourselves, but with Christ.

Though modern spirituality can take many forms, from overtly New Age teachings to more indistinct conglomerations of self-help practices and meditation, often the one common denominator is the focus on looking within oneself for answers, for truth, or even to discover deity. Yet Humphrey claims that counter to the "mantra of self-discovery" is the true cry central to the human condition: "for us to be delivered from ourselves by someone greater than ourselves."

SESSION 5: A SPIRITUALITY SMORGASBORD

- Humphrey calls the quest for an inner connection (promoted by cultural gurus like Oprah) "a truncated spirituality." What do you think she means by that? How is the Christian short-changed if his or her focus is personal or inward?

Read Paul's honest and brutal assessment of human nature in Romans 7:18–25.

- How do you think Paul would answer someone who thought ultimate spiritual fulfillment would come through a greater connection with oneself? What do you think he'd say?

Read Romans 8:1–11.

- List together the characteristics of the natural and spiritual states Paul describes. What are the differences in mind-set, behavior, and focus? What ultimately determines whether a person would be considered "natural" or "spiritual"?

CURRENT ISSUES: ENGAGING THE CULTURE

Humphrey asserts that as Christians, "When we speak of our human spirit being linked to the divine Spirit, that can only make sense in light of the particular one whose life, death, resurrection, and ascension have made it possible." She asserts that human beings become spiritual beings because of the work of Jesus Christ, "the life-giving spirit" (1 Corinthians 15:45).

- How have you experienced this to be true in your own life? How have you found fulfillment in connection with Christ that you would not find merely in connecting with yourself?

Christian spirituality flourishes through our interaction with the Holy Spirit.

Read Romans 8:11–16, 26–27. Humphrey writes that because of Christ's redeeming work, "A new potential for intimate fellowship with God . . . has been forged."

- How does this passage portray intimacy between Christians and God? Be specific.

- Which actions of the Holy Spirit stand out to you most from this passage? Why are they meaningful to you?

Humphrey concludes that "Christian spirituality is becoming present to the Lord, as he is always present to us."

- Imagine you were talking with a non-Christian friend who was into spirituality. How would you describe authentic Christian spirituality in your own words? How would you explain its distinction from popular spirituality?

■ Going Forward

- When have you felt attentive and "present" to the Lord recently? What was that experience like? What was the setting?

The seventeenth century monk Brother Lawrence penned a short treatise, *Practicing the Presence of God*. It detailed his effort to find God in his religious observances and in his private devotions. Ultimately, Brother Lawrence found he was better able to connect with God's presence in his everyday routine as he worked in the monastery kitchen. The monk simply attuned his heart to God's presence, having a secret conversation with him amid the clatter of pots and pans, while baking and washing dishes.

- Do you personally find it easy or challenging to stay focused on God's presence? Why do you think that's so? What practical steps might you take to grow in this practice?

- Humphrey says spirituality is the practice of "when or where or how the very Spirit of God meets with our spirits—both personally and corporately as the Body of Christ." In what ways can you grow in spirituality as a group? What habits can your group develop to "be present to the Lord" together?

■ Want to Explore More?

Recommended Resources

"The Divine Miss Winfrey," Ann Oldenburg, USA TODAY (www.usatoday.com/life/people/2006-05-10-oprah_x.htm)

You'll find a smattering of Oprah's tenets of spirituality in the "Spirit and Self" section of her Web site (http://www2.oprah.com/spiritself/ss_landing.jhtml)

Christian Spirituality: An Introduction, Alister E. MacGrath (Wiley-Blackwell, 1999: ISBN 0631212817)

Practicing the Presence of God, Brother Lawrence (Paraclete Press, 2007; ISBN 1557254656)

Satisfy Your Soul: Restoring the Heart of Christian Spirituality, Bruce Demarest (NavPress, 1999; ISBN 1576831302)

The Gospel According to Oprah, Marcia Z. Nelson (Westminster John Knox Press, 2005; ISBN 0664229425)

■ Notes

Is the church honestly a "counterculture for the common good"?

SCRIPTURE FOCUS

Matthew 5:21–22, 38–48; 23:25–28

Acts 2:42–47

PULLING WEEDS

IN THE CHURCH YARD

■

Most of us probably have a ready qualifier when unbelievers question us about faith issues—a way to distance ourselves from the often silly, and sometimes terrible, things perpetrated by so-called Christians. "Well, yes, I'm a Christian, but not like those abortion clinic bombers. And not like that CEO who defrauded his company. And not like . . . "

In the *Christianity Today* article "The Church's Great Malfunctions," Miroslav Volf writes, "Christian faith has been put to the most scandalous uses. As we reflect on how followers of Christ can exemplify 'a counterculture for the common good,' it's important to keep these ill effects of faith in mind." What should take the place of "idleness of faith and oppressiveness of faith," as Volf labels them? How can Christians address these "malfunctions" and weed them out? This study will discuss these issues.

■ Before You Meet

Read "The Church's Great Malfunctions" by Miroslav Wolf from *Christianity Today* magazine.

THE CHURCH'S GREAT MALFUNCTIONS

*We need to acknowledge these out of the deep
beauty and goodness of our faith.*

By Miroslav Volf

Though theology, like nearly every human endeavor, is a collaborative process, not many eminent theologians turn in articles with the names of co-authors attached. But Miroslav Volf's article arrived bearing no fewer than five additional names—Joseph Cumming, David Miller, Andrew Saperstein, Christian Scharen, and Travis Tucker, his colleagues at the Yale Center for Faith and Culture.

That generosity is a good clue to Volf's contribution to Christian theology. His 1996 book Exclusion and Embrace *was both a serious work of biblical and theological investigation and a deeply personal reflection on the horrors of sectarian violence in his native Croatia, setting a standard for personal engagement with its subject that theology, unfortunately, rarely meets.*

The Yale Center for Faith and Culture is dedicated to advancing faith as "a way of life," not just a way of thinking—a way that should transform every human practice. While the essay responds to the question we've been addressing in CT's 50th anniversary year—How can followers of Christ be a counterculture for the common good?—the Yale Center staff's collaboration is also an eloquent answer all by itself.

There is a remarkable image in the closing pages of Scripture that has become a touchstone for the way my colleagues and I think about faith and culture. Amid its descriptions of the New Jerusalem, Revelation includes "the tree of life, bearing twelve crops of fruit, yielding its fruit every month. And the leaves of the tree are for the healing of the nations" (Rev. 22:2 NIV). The tree holds out hope that whole cultures will be healed and mended, becoming places where people can flourish. And it sets an agenda for faith as a way of life that contributes to that flourishing, in anticipation, here and now.

Too often, however, Christian faith neither mends the world nor helps human beings thrive. To the contrary, it seems to shatter things into pieces, to choke what's new and beautiful before it has chance to take root, to trample underfoot what's good and true.

Some of faith's damaging effects are a matter of perspective. Prizing power, philosopher Friedrich Nietzsche derided Christianity for its "active sympathy for the ill-constituted and weak."

But even according to its own standards, Christian faith has been put to the most scandalous uses. As we reflect on how followers of Christ can exemplify "a counterculture for the common good," it's important to keep these ill effects of faith in mind. I'll call them "malfunctions" and group them under two rubrics: idleness of faith and oppressiveness of faith.

Spectacular Failure

He was a "good Christian man," he even taught Sunday school, and yet he ended up presiding over one of the worst business frauds in history, involving thousands of people and billions of dollars. I could be referring to any number of executives in the business-page headlines of the past several years, from Enron to WorldCom and beyond. Why didn't their faith prevent their crimes? I suspect at least three factors were at work in their faith's spectacular failure.

First, the *lure of temptation*. In a way, fraud in business is no different from infidelity in marriage or plagiarism in scholarly work. Even people committed to high moral standards succumb.

Giving in is as old as humanity—but so is victory over temptation. Virtuous character matters more than moral knowledge. Like Adam and Eve in the Fall or the self-confessing apostle Paul in Romans 7, most of those who do wrong know what's right but find themselves irresistibly attracted to evil. Faith idles when character shrivels.

Second, *the power of systems*. The lure of temptation is amplified by the power of the systems in which we work. This may be true most of all in the nearly ubiquitous market, whether that is the market of ideas, goods and services, political influence, or mass communication. More than a century ago, Max Weber spoke of the modern market as an "iron cage." The rules of the market demand that profit be maximized; these rules, and not moral considerations, determine how the game is played. Living as we inescapably do in various spheres that follow their own internal rules, we find ourselves leading divided lives.

Most people of faith living in the modern world have experienced the pull of divided loyalties. Though many have given in, many have also resisted by refusing to play by the rules of the game when those rules conflict with their deeply held convictions. They know they must be people of faith not only in the inner sanctuary of their souls, in their private lives, or when gathered with like-minded folks at church, but also in their everyday activities when scattered to the various places in which they do their daily work.

Third, a *misconstrued faith*. Karl Marx famously noted that religion—Christian faith, he primarily meant—is the "opiate of the people," a "downer" or depressant insulating them from reality and consoling them with a dream world of heavenly bliss. Marx missed the point that religion can often be an "upper," a stimulant that energizes people for tasks at hand. But the truth is that when Christian faith functions only as a soothing or performance-enhancing drug, that faith is, in fact, malfunctioning.

To be sure, the Christian Bible bears two great traditions that very roughly cover these two functions of faith, "deliverance" and "blessing." As deliverance, faith helps repair broken bodies and souls, including healing the wounds and disappointments inflicted on us. As blessing, faith energizes us to perform our tasks excellently, with requisite power, concentration, and creativity.

Yet if faith *only* heals and energizes, then it is merely a crutch, not a way of life. There are faiths of this sort—for example, mystical faiths of various kinds, including New Age spiritualities. But the Christian faith is not one of them. This faith does its proper work when it sets us on a journey, guides us along the way, and gives meaning to each step. When we embrace faith—when *God* embraces *us*—we become new creatures constituted and called to be part of the people of God. We are invited into the story of God's engagement with humanity. As we embark upon that journey, faith guides us by indicating paths to be taken and dark alleys to be avoided. Finally, faith's story gives meaning to all we do, from the smallest act to the weightiest. Is what we do in concord with that story? Then it is meaningful and will remain, glistening like corrosion-resistant gold. Does it clash with the story? Then it is ultimately meaningless and will burn like straw, even if we find it the most thrilling and fulfilling activity in which we've ever engaged.

For Christian faith not to be idle in the world, the work of doctors and garbage collectors, business executives and artists, stay-at-home moms or dads and scientists needs to be inserted into God's story with the world. That story needs to provide the most basic rules by which the game in all these spheres is played. And that story needs to shape the character of the players. I fear that few leaders in business, or in any field, think of their faith in those terms today.

Violent Faith

For Christians, faith is a precious good, the most valuable personal and social resource. When it is left untapped, the common good suffers—not just the particular interests of Christians. But many non-Christians today would consider the idleness of faith a minor blessing. Active faith is what they fear. As Sam Harris put it in *The End of Faith*, the Bible contains "mountains of life-destroying gibberish," and for Harris, when Christians take the Bible as their final authority, they act in violent, oppressive, life-destroying ways that undermine the common good.

A Serbian soldier rides on a tank and triumphantly flashes three fingers into the air—a symbol of the most holy Trinity, a sign that he belongs to a group that believes rightly about God. Clearly, his faith, in some sense, gives legitimacy to his triumphant ride on that killing machine. He's not alone in draping the wild-eyed god of war or the fierce goddess of nationalism with the legitimizing mantle of religious faith. Some of his Croatian enemies did the same, as have many Americans who eagerly merged the Cross and the flag. They follow in the footsteps of many Christians over the centuries who've left behind them a trail of blood and tears.

Consequently, critics say that by positing a cosmic struggle between good and evil, Christianity and other major religions are inescapably violent. Yet the absence of struggle against evil may bring more violence than the struggle itself, and not all struggle is properly described as violent. Critics say that monotheistic religions in particular divide the world into "us" (followers of the one true God) and "them" (followers of false idols). Yet polytheism divides people who worship incompatible gods into "us" and "them" even more fundamentally than does monotheism. Moreover, if we take the question of truth out of the sphere of religion, the only way to adjudicate competing claims of diverse gods is by violent struggle. And atheism did nothing to curtail the ravings of Stalin, Mao, or Pol Pot.

Christianity, of course, is not merely monotheism. And its particular claims about both divine reality and human history are a powerful resource for human flourishing. Critics can only see the death of the Son of God as divine child abuse, but Christians respond that Jesus Christ is not other *than* God but other *in* God. On the Cross, God takes the consequences of human sin on God's own divine self. The New Testament insists that such divine action provides the model for relations between human beings. Critics charge that Revelation's vision is one where a divine Rider kills all the enemies of God, but Christians are never encouraged in Revelation to imitate the Rider; to the contrary, they are told to imitate the martyrs—the *victims* of violence. Should not the violent, who persistently refuse to be redeemed by self-sacrificial love, be excluded from the final world of love? The "violence" of the divine Rider on the white horse is no more than the divine enactment of such exclusion.

So why have Christians, who embrace a peaceable faith, often been so violent? There are three main reasons, and they roughly correspond to the three reasons for faith's idleness.

First, a *thin faith*. Too many Christians embrace the ends mandated by their faith (for instance, maintaining the sanctity of unborn life or just social arrangements), but not the means by which faith demands that these ends be reached (persuasion rather than violence). The cure for religiously induced violence is not less faith but more faith—faith in its full scope, faith enacted with integrity and courage by its holy men and women, faith pondered responsibly by its great theologians.

Second, seemingly *irrelevant faith*. Can a faith born two thousand years ago tell us anything useful about democratic governance, running a modern corporation, or defending a nation from terrorists? Sensing a tension, we use faith merely to bless what we think is right to do. It takes hard intellectual and spiritual work to learn to understand and live faith authentically under changed circumstances. This work cannot be placed only on the shoulders of theologians; it must be an endeavor in which faithful people from all walks of life are engaged, and study of a variety of disciplines must be involved.

Finally, *unwillingness to walk the narrow path*. Often "impractical" slides into "overly demanding." Someone has violated us or our community; we feel the urge for revenge—and we set aside the explicit command to love our enemies, to be benevolent and beneficent toward them. Or we believe that our culture is going down a perilous road; we want to change its self-destructive course—and we forget that the ends that Christian faith holds high do not justify setting aside its strictures about the appropriate means.

And so we're back at the question of character. In addition to applying an authentically understood faith to various spheres of life, we need properly formed persons who resist misusing faith in oppressive ways. For the Christian faith produces devastating results when it devolves into a mere personal or cultural resource for people whose lives, like the life of that Serbian soldier, may be guided by anything but that faith.

The Task Ahead

Is it really possible for our faith to become functional again in spite of these two great and troubling malfunctions? Only if we expose the malfunctions with the honesty of those who know that our salvation doesn't depend on our moral excellence. We Christians should be our own most rigorous critics—and be that precisely out of a deep sense of the beauty and goodness of our faith.

Then we can begin to think of faith neither as simply a system of propositions to be believed, nor as merely a set of energizing and healing techniques to be practiced, but as an integral way of life. This will not take the form of a free-floating "public theology" unrelated to concrete communities of faith. The Christian pursuit of the common good must be church-based without being church-centered. We need to build and strengthen mature communities of vision and character who celebrate faith as a way of life as they gather before God for worship and who, sent by God, live it out as they scatter to pursue various tasks in the world.

In all of this, we will do well to learn from non-Christian endeavors. A temptation for any group that sees itself as a counterculture is to understand its relation to society in oppositional terms. But blanket opposition isn't right for those who believe in God as the source of all truth, goodness, and beauty. We do not need to melt down all the gold of the Egyptians. While some non-Christian approaches may have to be rejected, others can be taken over as they are, and still others repaired or improved. As a counterculture, we work for the common good—because we believe in the common grace of the one God.

Miroslav Volf serves as Director of the Yale Center for Faith and Culture and is the Henry B. Wright Professor of Systematic Theology at Yale Divinity School.

("The Church's Great Malfunctions" was first published in *Christianity Today*, October 2006)

For more insightful articles from *Christianity Today* magazine, visit http://www. ctlibrary.com/ and subscribe now.

■ Open Up

Select one of these activities to launch your discussion time.

Option 1

Discuss one of these icebreaker questions:

- When has a Christian public figure or a Christian organization made you feel "proud" to be a Christian? Explain.

- When have the actions of a Christian public figure or a Christian organization caused you to feel embarrassed or ashamed? Give an example.

- How do you usually react when non-Christians talk to you about the latest moral failure of a Christian in the public eye, or violence perpetrated in the name of Christ?

Option 2

Divide into two groups; each group needs a poster board (or piece of paper) and a marker. Each group should work together to complete your assignment below:

Group 1: Draw a picture of a church; next to your picture, list words or phrases that represent how Christians view the church. What should it be? What is it actually like? What does it mean in the lives of Christians (like yourself)?

Group 2: How do you think most non-Christians view the church? Draw a picture of a church building, representing it from a non-Christian perspective. Then list words or phrases (both positive and negative) that represent how you think non-Christians view the church.

Get back together and share your posters, then talk about how you've encountered these contrasting viewpoints in your own life.

■ The Issue

Faith in Jesus is meant to be, according to Scripture, a way of life that presents hope and healing to individuals and cultures. "Too often, however," Miroslav Volf writes in his article, "Christian faith neither mends the world nor helps human beings thrive. To the contrary, it seems to shatter things into pieces, to choke up what's new and beautiful before it has a chance to take root, to trample underfoot what's good and true." Ouch!

Volf suggests that there are two main "malfunctions" within the church. The first is "idleness of faith," where, because of temptation, compartmentalized lives, and misconstrued thinking about Christ, Christians view faith as an enhancement drug rather than a reality in which to live our whole lives. The result is moral failure.

The second malfunction is "oppressiveness of faith." Volf states that these Christians have embraced the "ends" of faith but not the Christ-like "means"; they view faith as irrelevant to modern issues and find it too demanding to live the values of the kingdom. Thus, Christians can resort to oppressive, at times violent, methods to accomplish their goals. "We Christians should be our most rigorous critics," Volf writes. This will lead the way towards a mature way of life—a "counterculture for the common good."

- Do you agree with Volf that these are the two great malfunctions of the modern church? Did he miss any? Did he over/understate the ones he chose?

- How have you experienced these malfunctions in your own life?

■ Reflect

Take a moment to read Matthew 5:21–22, 38–48; 23:25–28; and Acts 2:42–47 on your own. Jot down a few notes and observations about these passages: In what ways do these teachings relate to the article you read? What questions do these passages bring up for you? What are the key ideas that stand out to you?

■ Let's Explore

Real faith is an integrated reality, not an idle veneer.

• Think of recent examples of self-professed Christians who've failed morally in a public way. Volf asks, "Why didn't their faith prevent their crimes?" What's your answer to that?

Theologian Dallas Willard, in *The Divine Conspiracy*, writes tongue-in-cheek:

> The theology of Christian trinkets says there is something about the Christian that works like the bar code . . . Some belief or some association with a group affects God the way the bar code affects the scanner. Perhaps there has occurred a moment of mental assent to a creed . . . God "scans" it, and forgiveness floods forth. An appropriate amount of righteousness is shifted from Christ's account to our account . . . We are accordingly "saved" . . . How could we not be Christians?

The kingdom of God, however, is a transforming reality that we are invited to live in, not simply a label, badge, or sweet candy coating.

• Read Matthew 23:25–28. These are strong words. Why do you think Jesus is so harsh? What does this passage tell you about the kind of faith that Jesus values?

- What are some ways people tend to "clean the outside of the cup" or "whitewash tombs"? In ways have you felt tempted to focus on the outward appearance of faith? Share specific examples you've encountered or experienced.

- How does one clean the "inside of the cup"? What practices or experiences have helped you grow in integrating your inner faith and your outer life?

Real faith is a call to love enemies, not a violent oppressiveness.

Christian faith has been used to justify acts as violent as the Crusades, the lynching of blacks in America, and the bombing of abortion clinics. And maybe not as violent—but certainly as vicious—can be the rhetoric Christians use in public political and moral debates. However, faith requires Christ followers to put ourselves under the Word of God, not the other way around.

- Volf identifies three factors that lead to an oppressive faith: a thin faith, an irrelevant faith, and an unwillingness to walk the narrow path. What do these terms mean to you? How have you observed these factors in the church?

- Read Matthew 5:21–22, 38–48. In what ways do churches and followers of Christ sometimes practice the old law of "Love your neighbor and hate your enemy" (v. 43) today? Are you guilty of this?

- Many of us may feel that we don't have any "enemies"—yet there are certainly people in our lives whom we find challenging to love. How would you describe the new standard Jesus sets in this passage in your own words? How should that new standard look like in relation to:

— Those whose personalities grate against our own?

— Those whose political views conflict with our own?

— Those whose religious ideas contradict our own?

— Those whose ethnic heritage or cultural background is different from our own?

— Those who are literal "enemies"—people who've personally hurt us or people in nations with whom our country is at war?

Real faith is expressed in an authentic community that influences the surrounding world as a "counterculture for the common good."

- Read Acts 2:42–47. What inspires you about this description of the early church? Do you think this kind of community would prevent some of the malfunctions we see in the modern church? Why or why not?

- Volf suggests that the "Christian pursuit of the common good must be church-based without being church-centered." What do you think that means? How would it look in your church community?

■ Going Forward

- What's one "malfunction" you feel is prevalent in your church congregation? How will you personally strive to help your church grow in that area? Share specific ideas or action steps.

Break into pairs to read and discuss the following:

It's easy to critique "the church" when we're thinking in terms of *other* people. But we are each *part* of "the church" and it's essential that we turn the magnifying glass on to ourselves.

"The unexamined life is not worth living," the Greek philosopher Socrates observed. So true; but what he forgot to mention is that the unexamined life doesn't do much good for those who come in contact with it either. Reactionary, self-righteous lives tend to leave a trail of broken and ignored people behind them. But regular and honest examination of our faith in light of Christ's values and methods will allow us to extend hope and healing to the world.

Volf writes: "We Christians should be our own most rigorous critics . . . We need to build and strengthen mature communities of vision and character who celebrate faith as a way of life. . . . . As a counterculture, we work for the common good—because we believe in the common grace of the one God."

- Be your own "most rigorous critic" for a moment. What is one specific way you've felt challenged by Scripture or by your discussion during this study?

Conclude by gathering back together as a group and sharing a time of repentance. Share honestly with each other, as you feel led, how you feel convicted about issues of idleness and oppressiveness, and the factors that lead to them (the lure of temptation, a misconstrued faith, or an unwillingness to walk the narrow path). Of whom do you need to ask forgiveness? Have you failed in your faith or character? Is there some person or group that you are oppressive toward in your language or actions?

After you share, pray together, accepting God's forgiveness and seeking his help as you grow in faith and spiritual maturity.

■ Want to Explore More?

Recommended Resources

Churches That Make a Difference: Reaching Your Community With Good News & Good Works, Ronald J. Sider, Philip N. Olson, Heidi Rolland Unruh (Baker Books, 2002; ISBN 0801091330)

Exclusion and Embrace: A Theological Exploration of Identity, Otherness, and Reconciliation, Miroslav Volf (Abingdon Press, 1996; ISBN 0687002826)

God's Politics: A New Vision for Faith & Politics in America, Jim Wallis (Harper SanFrancisco, 2005; ISBN 0060558288)

Practicing Theology: Beliefs and Practices in the Christian Life, Miroslav Volf and Dorothy C. Bass, editors (Wm. B. Eerdmans Publishing Company, 2001; ISBN 0802849318)

Renovation of the Heart: Putting on the Character of Christ, Dallas Willard (NavPress, 2002; ISBN 1576832961)

The Divine Conspiracy: Rediscovering Our Hidden Life in God, Dallas Willard (Harper SanFrancisco, 1998; ISBN 0060693339)

How can we maintain a vibrant faith in the midst of comfort, consumerism, and clutter?

SCRIPTURE FOCUS

Matthew 11:28–30

Romans 5:1–5

Hebrews 10:19–25

THE DREAM LIFE?

■

In "Suburban Spirituality," Dave Goetz examines the life and mind-set of a typical American suburbanite. It's a lifestyle that can easily lead to spiritual complacency—or, at the other extreme, a spiritual restlessness characterized by chronic church-hopping, forever seeking the one with the latest "buzz." The trends he observes in suburbia pervade our culture and influence urban and rural environments as well. In this study, we'll examine what Scripture has to say about lifestyles focused on comfort, driven by consumerism, and overwhelmed by clutter.

■ Before You Meet

Read "Suburban Spirituality" by David Goetz from *Christianity Today* magazine.

SUBURBAN SPIRITUALITY

The land of SUVs and soccer leagues tends to weather the soul in peculiar ways, but it doesn't have to.

By David Goetz

The SUV in the driveway, the golden retriever with a red bandana romping with two children in the front yard, the Colorado winter vacations, the bumper sticker with "My daughter is an honor roll student at Hubble Middle School"—those are the dreams of the denizens, like me, of suburbia.

After college and their roaring twenties, many Americans find themselves in a subdivision with a lawn and a mortgage and a couple kids. Hip twentysomethings may mock the suburbs and its bourgeois values, but when their first child arrives, the nesting instinct sets in. A neighbor and her husband lived on the north side of Chicago until the kids came; then they moved to a western 'burb for safety and quiet. "I miss the energy of the city," she says five years later. "In fact, when we moved to the suburbs, we had a hard time sleeping at night because the neighborhood was so quiet."

Such deep quiet is how suburbs were originally conceived. The architecture of today's rolling acres of spec houses in farmlands arises in part from the pastoral, bucolic cemeteries on the outskirts of cities in the early part of the 20th century. Whether blue-collar or white-collar, Yankee or Southern, West Coast or East, North Dakota or southern Texas, most 'burbs are arguably organized around the provision of safety and opportunities for children, and neat and tranquil environs for homeowners. Suburbs have grown to dominate the American landscape precisely because, most of the time, they fulfill those promises, in spades. That very success presents challenges for Christians.

Naturally, there are exceptions. There are suburbs just as plagued by poverty and crime as inner cities. But in this essay, whenever I refer to the suburbs, I will be speaking to what I know: cozy, safe, homogeneous, fairly affluent suburbia.

In the introduction to *Crabgrass Frontier*, sociologist Kenneth T. Jackson writes, "[T]he space around us—the physical organization of neighborhoods, roads, yards, houses, and apartments—sets up living patterns that condition our behavior." I grew up in a rural setting and moved as a young adult to the suburbs, and what Jackson observed sociologically I've concluded must also be true spiritually.

The environment of the suburbs weathers one's soul peculiarly. That is, there is an environmental variable, mostly invisible, that oxidizes the Christian spirit, like the metal of a car in the elements.

The pop artist Jewel, a young woman in her middle twenties whose albums have sold millions, talked several years ago with *Rolling Stone* magazine about her motivations. She said, "I'm just a person who is honestly trying to live my life and asking, 'How do you be spiritual and live in the world without going to a monastery?'"

Her question rattled around in my brain, for neither can I move to a monastery. I'm stuck in the 'burbs; I don't have easy access to nature (that is, enough cash flow to afford a second house in some rural area), to quiet, to a more contemplative life. Something deep within me yearns for a more spacious spiritual consciousness, a more direct connection to the God of the galaxies. How can I draw close to my Creator in a world of endless strip malls, cookie-cutter houses, ubiquitous vans and sport-utility vehicles, and no space for solitude? A colleague calls the Chicago suburbs "the land of no horizons." Power lines, the dormers on a neighbor's Cape Cod, and mature hardwoods obstruct the full evening's redness in the west. The day's final beauty is always about an hour away. I commute to the country to see the stars.

Some days I fantasize about moving my family from our western Chicago suburb to a small town in the western United States, edged by a rambling stream and cradled in the foothills of a mountain range with a romantic name like the Spanish Peaks. There we'd live out our days in simplicity and in natural beauty and with few financial anxieties.

Life would be fully aligned. Our frenetic life would slow to a manageable pace, and God would be easier to access.

But I know that what glistens in my mind is a phantasm; I know what small towns are like. I grew up in mostly rural communities whose most notable architectural landmarks were the county courthouse and the Tastee-Freez and whose citizens suffered from poverty and isolation. My high school class numbered seventeen. At least in the North and South Dakota prairie soil in which I was seeded and sprouted, God did not seem nearer because of the environment. And if beauty and solitude are preliminary to the deeper life, then why does the mountain state region have the highest suicide rate in the United States? What good, then, is creation?

While I esteem the saints throughout Christian history who abandoned the cities to draw close to God, most living in the suburbs and cities can't follow them. A few can, but for most people, family and career choices obviate a more contemplative life. If the get-away-from-it-all model of Christian spirituality is the high road, then most ordinary suburban folk, wedged in cloned subdivisions, can follow Christ only in lowly cul-de-sacs.

While I can't afford to evacuate my family, I occasionally feel a twinge of disease with my comforts. DuPage County, in which I live, ranks in the top 10 percent of counties in America with the highest household income. I'm not completely distracted from how the rest of the world lives. I have noticed the hidden peoples of my white-collar county—the refugees from Zaire and Bosnia, and the Indian and Asian students at the local community college. Yet despite the best the 'burbs have to offer my family—security, options, and efficiency—I find myself restless, always pursuing, always striving, finding less and less fulfillment. I don't seem to need simply another Bible study or another church service to find soul satisfaction. My faith often seems to have no effect on my anxiety.

In the opening paragraphs of *The Message in the Bottle,* Walker Percy asked:

Why does man feel so sad in the twentieth century? . . . Why do people often feel bad in good environments and good in bad environments? Why do people often feel so bad in good environments that they prefer bad environments? . . . Why is it that a man riding a good commuter train from Larchmont to New York, whose needs and drives are satisfied, who has a good home, loving wife and family, good job, who enjoys unprecedented "cultural and recreational facilities," often feels bad without knowing why?

In good environments like mine, many spend their lives paying mortgages for homes in subdivisions with names such as "Klein Creek," "Mill Creek," "Highlands Ranch," and "Pinehurst"—euphemisms for rows of uniform houses of pressboard siding, regardless of square footage, in which stressed-out, tired, weary souls reside.

But the 'burbs are where I live—and I have set about to discover the life Jesus describes at the end of Matthew 11: "Keep company with me and you'll learn to live freely and lightly" (MSG).

Suburban church consumerism has been lamented for years. Rural churches suffer from consumerism as well, but deeper family ties may prevent some of the extreme forms of church mobility seen in the suburbs. My point throughout this essay is not that the hazards of upper middle-class suburbia can't be found elsewhere. But to me, they seem to be intensified in my white-collar community. At any rate, this is the geography in which I find myself, and the examples here naturally arise out of this geography.

Where I live, a church building seems to fill at least one corner of every major intersection. And on Sunday, many high school auditoriums are rented by start-up churches. There is no shortage of places to worship. With so many choices, some change churches like they change dry cleaners. One person candidly told me that at least part of the reason he and his family evacuated one suburb and shuttled their possessions another ten miles west was that they "weren't getting fed" by their pastor. By buying a house in a suburb thirty minutes away, they could more tastefully explain to their church friends their reason for leaving: "We needed a church closer to our new home."

Church migration patterns tend to follow whatever church has the "buzz"—the "biblical" preacher, the new contemporary service, the nuevo liturgical service, the acoustical, postmodern service, the youth ministry with the great weekend retreats and exotic mission trips. Choice is a beautiful thing.

I too tend to be flighty. I'd probably change churches every couple years, if it weren't for my wife and the fact that almost sixty years ago her father helped start the church we attend. A few months after we migrated to Chicago in the early 1990s, Jana and I drove in a cold spring rain to Door County, Wisconsin, a beautiful, timbered resort area, for a Memorial Weekend jaunt. We hoped the weekend would warm up, but things grew icy when I made a flippant remark about "her church." Our recent move put us in Jana's hometown, and we were in the process of deciding where to attend church. I knew that once Jana and I began attending "her" church, her long history there would lash us to it and restrict my freedom to circulate in the extended body of Christ. The covert pressure I felt from Jana and her family irked me, and I knew how such comments irked my wife.

We finally settled on Jana's home church, which we attend to this day. But for all my early carping, the commitment to this one church has forced me to develop spiritually.

In *The Four Loves*, C. S. Lewis points out that nature, for all its staggering beauty, is limited for the seeker of God; natural beauty can't communicate God's truths about salvation and about the contemplative life of following Christ. "Nature cannot satisfy the desires she arouses nor answer theological questions nor sanctify us. Our real journey to God involves constantly turning our backs on her; passing from the dawn-lit fields into some pokey little church, or (it might be) going to work in an East End Parish."

For all of its foibles—which at its worst include lousy preaching, political infighting, self-centeredness, stagnation, a gaggle of special-interest groups—the poky local church in suburbia is still the most fertile environment for spiritual development there. Genuine spiritual progress doesn't happen without a long-term attachment to a poky local church. I'm all for improving the organization of a local church to make it more biblically effective, but the maddening frustration that prompts someone to leave one church for another may be the precise thing that holds great potential for spiritual progress—if one stays. "Just as surely as God desires to lead us to a knowledge of genuine Christian fellowship, so surely must we be overwhelmed by a great disillusionment with others, with Christians in general, and, if we are fortunate, with ourselves," Dietrich Bonhoeffer wrote. "Only that fellowship which faces such disillusionment, with all its unhappy and ugly aspects, begins to be what it should be in God's sight, begins to grasp in faith the promise that is given to it."

Disillusionment with one's church, then, is not a reason to leave but a reason to stay and see what God will create in one's life and in the local church. What I perceive to be my needs—"I need a church with a more biblical preacher who uses specific examples from real life"—may not correspond to my true spiritual needs. Often I am not attuned to my true spiritual needs. Thinking that I know my true needs is arrogant and narcissistic. Staying put as a life practice allows God's grace to work on the unsanded surfaces of my inner life. Seventeenth-century French Catholic mystic François Fénelon wrote, "Slowly you will learn that all the troubles in your life—your job, your health, your inward failings—are really cures to the poison of your old nature."

I would add "your church" to his list; that is, all the troubles in one's church are really cures to the poison of one's old nature, or, as the Apostle Paul put it in Romans 7, the "sinful nature." The biggest problem in any church I attend is myself—and my love of self and my penchant to roam when I sense my needs aren't being met.

Staying put and immersing oneself in the life of a gathered community forces one into eventual conflict with other church members, with church leadership, or with both. Frustration and conflict are the raw materials of spiritual development. All the popular reasons given for shopping for another church are actually spiritual reasons for staying put. They are a means of grace, preventing talk of spirituality from becoming sentimental or philosophical. Biblical spirituality is earthy, face-to-face, and often messy.

In a congregational meeting, two young male professionals made a presentation to update the sanctuary sound system. There was some tension in the air, because the system was pricey. They delivered their pitch well and then began fielding questions. A retired man, a former physician, challenged one presenter's use of a technical term. I don't remember the exact phrasing that sparked the fireworks, but the young presenter and this retired doctor began to quarrel about who was right, as if they were the only two in the room. I felt embarrassed for the older man, since his comment and persistence provoked and sustained the interchange. The discussion ended awkwardly, the congregation voting to upgrade the sound system, and the meeting came to a close. Afterward, I saw the elderly man amble toward the presenters. Later I heard that the retired physician had apologized for his conduct and asked one of the young professionals out for breakfast to discuss the sound system.

At its best, the local church functions as an arena in which conflict and hurts among participants who choose to stay can open up possibilities for spiritual progress. Where else will people still accept me after I stand up in a church meeting and harshly criticize something? "Ah, that's just Dave," they say. They know me. I learn about the Christian virtues of acceptance and graciousness even as I am not accepting and gracious. By not taking my toys and playing elsewhere—that is, finding a church that connects with my spiritual journey—I move forward in my spiritual journey. I give up control. I forfeit my options in an environment of choices.

Norman Maclean of the University of Chicago probably never imagined that his book *A River Runs Through It* (University of Chicago Press, 1976) would trigger a flood of upper-middle-class, suburban white males to his sport. Fly-fishing is almost a cliché now in suburban life—one of the best fly shops in the Midwest is a couple miles from my house in dead-center suburbia.

In the sport of fly-fishing, the primary goal is to cast into the stream or river an imitation of a bug so it appears to be real—a real mosquito or ant or grasshopper or mayfly. The trout spies the imitation rolling along the bottom of the stream or suspended in it or floating on its surface, and strikes.

If fishing under the surface with a "wet fly," the fly-fisher must at all times pay attention to how the lure appears under the surface. The fly-fisher, who can't see the fly because it's under the water, must watch the floating fly line as it drifts with the current. The fly-fisher's goal is to cast upstream and then let the fly float downstream in a "dead drift," in which the imitation insect flows along with the current as naturally as possible. This is painfully difficult to execute.

To create a dead drift, the fly-fisher mends the fly-line as the fly floats downstream. Mending is one of the key activities in effective fly-fishing. The current, uneven across any given stretch of river, pulls the line unevenly, eventually pulling at the fly under the water. The fly-fisher must periodically flip only the line that lies on the surface (tossing it either forward or back, depending on how the line bows), thus creating slack so the fly beneath can continue to ride naturally with the current. The better one is at mending, the better the results.

Mending may be a key image for spiritual development in the suburbs, to "experience the depths of Jesus Christ," as the classic work by Jeanne Guyon, the 17th-century Christian mystic, put it. The trick for the lover of God is to learn how to become better at mending one's life, to make small adjustments on a regular basis in order to avoid the speed and clutter of modern living.

It seems that every child in the more affluent suburbs is tagged—talented and gifted. The environmental pressures to nurture children toward success tend to bloat one's life: park district soccer, tee-ball, swimming. Then the traveling leagues, clubs, drama, youth group outings. Finally special classes or tutors to prepare for the SAT. The covert pressure is to move upward in housing, friends, "educational opportunities" (for example, spring break family trips to Paris), and vacations.

Several friends and acquaintances have left their suburban life for a three-month or yearlong stint as missionaries. When they return, their faces flush from life abroad, often they downscale their lifestyles, strangely energized. Some return to buy homes with lower mortgages. But I've often noticed that the experience eventually wears off, like a summer tan in early fall. At least outwardly, they appear as before—fully engaged in the busyness of suburban life.

Entropy is nowhere more at work than in one's spiritual energy and good intentions. That's especially true in the suburbs, where the accumulation of activities drives one to exhaustion. Mending reverses this—making small adjustments to our life, constantly paring back that which gloms onto our life in the natural ebb and flow of making life work.

My wife and I have been mentored by an older couple, who in their mid-sixties moved from their nice suburban house to an upscale retirement community nearby—a normal migration pattern for economically free seniors. It's a kind of mending—adjusting their lifestyle to less home and thus less work. But often it doesn't work that way.

The wife, after moving to the retirement community, couldn't sleep at night. "I kept thinking of all the money it took to heat this place." It was the best of the best. They chose the retirement home because of its amenities—and their intentions were noble: the husband worried that his wife might end up with senile dementia, which haunts her family history. The upscale amenities were a hedge against the future. But after only a short time, the couple decided to back out of their agreement—and took a huge financial loss—because they felt convicted by the high monthly fee. As the wife says, "We didn't belong there. We could afford it, but we couldn't."

Then they moved to a smaller townhouse complex, purchased two units, and used one for living and the other as a home for missionary families on furlough. Their friends clucked, "They must be having financial problems." Even in their mid-sixties, they felt peer pressure. But their mending freed up their minds and life.

A young family I know sold their weekend home—because commuting more than four hours to enjoy it created not rest but anxiety. Others strip themselves of all church responsibilities after a season of intense involvement, to reorder their lives. The Epistles of John often use the present tense in such verbs as "abide" to denote continual action—also called the continual present. Mending is a verb and a life practice that opens us up to the free and light life offered by Christ.

In my mid-twenties, I cobbled together a living in the Denver metro area, part of what's known as the Front Range, where eastern Colorado's thinly grassed plains give way to foothills and then to the Rocky Mountains. During the harsh light of midday, if a traveler driving westward from Kansas to Colorado along Interstate 70 gazes toward the foothills and mountains, the landscape appears one-dimensional, flat, like the false storefronts of an old Western movie.

But in the softer, changing light of dusk, the foothills and mountains separate and emerge and fatten, take form. As darkness falls, the shadows lengthen and accentuate the canyons and flat irons and ridges. The landscape becomes multidimensional. The escaping light gives the traveler depth of field, a deeper, truer grasp of reality: the landscape is not at all flat; it's thick, layered, deep.

A spiritual life lived well is a life lived in the thickness—in the space beyond and including the three-dimensional form of the moment. But it's this fatness or richness of life that we often obviate by striving to advance in our career, move to the bigger house, get our student a soccer scholarship, make sure our kids get in the tag program.

"The higher goal of spiritual living is not to amass a wealth of information, but to face sacred moments," Abraham Heschel writes in *The Sabbath*. "[I]t is not a thing that lends significance to a moment; it is a moment that lends significance to things."

Often, suffering forces the significance. A friend's forty-year-old brother collapsed in a Foot Locker retail store, the news gutting her life. She lived the dream: three beautiful, well-adjusted kids, the sprawling house in a new subdivision, her husband on the corporate dole. After the funeral, weeks later, one of her friends brought over some photos of a beautiful, early winter afternoon. The photos showed her children, happy, bundled, joyful. She looked at the date on the photos. The time was the exact moment her brother had died—only she didn't know it at the time, of course, while the photos were being snapped. The phone call came several hours after.

Later she said, "While my life was merrily happening, it was also changing, in ways I could never imagine."

That is the true nature of life; we try to control it and in the process it controls us, picking us up randomly, like a tornado, and dropping us into a foreign place. So much of suburban life seems to be about preventing the tornado, an act as ridiculous as controlling an incoming storm. Isn't feeling safe in case of accident or storm the reason most folks buy SUVs? But no SUV can prevent the call from the police in the middle of the night. Or the news from an unfaithful spouse. Or the sudden heart attack. Or depression. Or kids who have it.

My point is not about what one drives. Others can moralize about the economics and politics of SUVs. I'm trying to identify a much larger, unchallenged assumption about life that seems to prevail in, though it's not limited to, the suburbs—that with more effort and organization, life can become sure. I've often wondered if that's why poverty and suffering hide more easily in the neat-looking suburbs. To admit to a less than perfect life is to betray the tacit code of honor that we all agree to when we buy that first house in the Pine Hills subdivision.

Other than my frequent business commutes into downtown Chicago, the only time I brush up against poverty is when I patronize the local Starbucks coffee shop in its western suburb of Glen Ellyn. On a park bench just down the sidewalk from the shop, I often encounter a street person—often the same person—staring blankly at Lands' End couples with babies heading for a latté and biscotti. I've even bought this senior citizen a cup of decaf, the house blend (when she wasn't already holding one donated from another guilt-ridden local).

In the rural environments in which I grew up, poverty didn't hide as well, and opulence was less conspicuous. Or was it more conspicuous? Perhaps we didn't feel as if the life of the wealthy were just beyond our grasp. In the countryside, as in many urban environments, much of life stands in stark relief to itself, and the nature of life and death is more accepted. Perhaps rural inhabitants have a more intrinsic knowledge about the ritual of death—the slaughter of chickens and cattle—a deeper understanding of the bloody cycle of life. Many farmers weather years short on cash and long on debt, subsisting on borrowed money, even for groceries. In many smaller rural communities, even as large as Bozeman, Montana (a community of about thirty thousand), landing a job at Wal-Mart may mean a buck or so above minimum wage and health insurance.

But suffering is no respecter of environments. It's not that suburbanites don't suffer as much as rural or city folks, but that perhaps we struggle more to deny suffering's reality. But no matter how we hedge against the future, the transitory nature of life gets revealed.

And sometimes we have to go out of our way to have it revealed. One way to confront this denial is as old as the Christian faith: voluntarily entering into the suffering of others. For some it's a weekly or monthly visit to a nursing home. For others it's taking into their homes foster children or pregnant teenagers for short stints. For one friend, it has been volunteering at the local homeless shelter.

My friend says this has not been a radically transforming spiritual experience. For a few years, he carped about how the interchurch homeless ministry relegates evangelism to the periphery, how it has aggravated homelessness by treating the homeless as guests, and so on. But in the course of working breakfast, dinner, and midnight shifts, he's learned to let go of his preconceptions of "successful homeless ministry" and begin to simply learn to *be with* the homeless. His most rewarding moments come after breakfast is served and he stands with the smokers outdoors in the patio, talking with them, mostly just listening to their stories—often narcissistic and far-fetched tales of injustices visited upon them, but sometimes poignant narratives of lives gone terribly awry. "I'm still not very good at entering into their suffering," he says, "but my life is so sheltered with material blessings and psychologically healthy friends, it's better than nothing. At least once a month, I'm forced to think about those who genuinely suffer."

And as Scripture and church history teach, wherever there is suffering, there is God, and by not avoiding or ignoring it, we embrace it—and live life in full color.

Haddon Robinson, professor of preaching at Gordon-Conwell Theological Seminary, once said that change often comes about like this: pain + time + insight = change. Life practices like these, and others, may return to me, a middle-aged suburban male, the gift of God himself. Poking fun at Mayberry is a cliché, but it turns out that the trimmed and bucolic cul de sac is no better or worse a place to work out one's salvation with fear and trembling.

David Goetz is founder and president of cz Marketing, a marketing management firm and author of Death by Suburb: How to Keep the Suburbs From Killing Your Soul. *He has been an editor at* Leadership, *CT's sister publication for pastors.*

("Suburban Spirituality" was first published in *Christianity Today*, July 2003, Page 30.)

For more insightful articles from *Christianity Today* magazine, visit http://www.ctlibrary.com/ and subscribe now.

■ Open Up

Select one of these activities to launch your discussion time.

Option 1

Discuss these icebreaker questions:

- Describe "the American dream." What does it look like in terms of possessions and achievements? What feelings do people associate with it?

- Which elements of the "the American dream" are truly good, meaningful, or fulfilling? How have you experienced these in your own life?

- Which elements of the American dream are false and unfulfilling? Give examples.

Option 2

Collect several recent magazines (news, sports, entertainment, or pop culture magazines). In pairs or individually, leaf through a magazine and tear out images and advertisements that epitomize the modern "American dream."

After a few minutes, spread out all the pages and talk about your observations:

• What common images or ideas do you see?

• What's appealing about these things?

■ The Issue

In "Suburban Spirituality," David Goetz quotes pop star Jewel in a Rolling Stone interview: "I'm just a person who is honestly trying to live my life and asking, 'How do you be spiritual and live in the world without going to a monastery?'"

• Can you relate to that question? How would you define the perfect environment for spiritual growth? Would it be a monastery?

Goetz zeroes in on life for a Christian in the suburbs, saying that environment "weathers one's soul peculiarly. That is, there is an environmental variable, mostly invisible, that oxidizes the Christian spirit, like the metal of a car in the elements." He builds upon Jewel's question, asking, "How can I draw close to my Creator in a world of endless strip malls, cookie-cutter houses, ubiquitous vans and sport-utility vehicles, and no space for solitude?"

- Can you relate to Goetz? From your experience (in the suburbs or a different setting), what is it about everyday life that hinders one's spiritual quest for a vibrant faith?

■ Reflect

Take a moment to read Matthew 11:28–30; Romans 5:1–5; and Hebrews 10:19–25 on your own. Jot down a few notes and observations about the passages: What appear to be the main ideas in each passage? Which particular words or phrases stand out to you? What questions do these passages bring up?

■ Let's Explore

Though our culture prizes choice and consumerism, a vibrant faith values commitment to one's "poky local church."

We live in a culture saturated with choice—just spend some time in the cereal aisle of a grocery store for an example. We're used to taking our pick—scrutinizing, selecting, and then getting exactly what we want. Unfortunately, this mind-set can easily bleed into our perspective on the local church (hence the consumerism-laden phrase "church shopping"). In many locales, churches of all worship styles and theological stripes abound. "With so many choices," Goetz observes, "some [people] change churches like they change dry cleaners."

- How have you observed a trend among Christians "to follow whatever church has the 'buzz'"? What are some of the most common reasons for church-hopping (leaving one church for another)? Do you think these reasons are legitimate?

- When have you felt disillusioned or frustrated with your local church? How did you respond?

Read Hebrews 10:19–25. In this passage written to Christians facing severe persecution, the author urges his readers to maintain a very high level of commitment to each other—both practically (meeting together) and spiritually (spurring one another on).

- What do you think these early Christians would say about modern-day church hopping?

Sticking it out in a church community will inevitably mean working through frustrating or even painful situations. But those tough aspects of community-life can also spur one on in faith. Goetz goes so far as to say, "Genuine spiritual progress doesn't happen without a long-term attachment to a poky local church." He quotes Dietrich Bonhoeffer: "Just as surely as God desires to lead us to a knowledge of genuine Christian fellowship, so surely must we be overwhelmed by great disillusionment with others, with Christians in general, and, if we are fortunate, with ourselves."

- Have you experienced what it's like to be part of a local church for a long time? If so, how did your attachment to that group help you grow? If not, what do you think you've missed out on?

Though our culture promotes a cluttered lifestyle, a vibrant faith chooses to make time and space for sacred moments.

Perhaps one of the greatest hallmarks of our culture is our tendency to cram more and more "stuff" into our lives, amassing a preponderance of possessions and accumulating more and more activities in our schedule. This obtrusive clutter can easily crowd out any room to breathe and leave us exhausted.

- When have you felt like your life is full of "clutter"? What are some of the key sources of clutter in your life (possessions, activities, or other)?

Read Matthew 11:28–30. In *The Message*, Eugene Peterson renders Jesus's words in verse 30 this way: "Keep company with me and you'll learn to live freely and lightly."

- Describe a cluttered lifestyle typical in our culture. Next, describe a way of living that is light and free—a lifestyle that allows space for "sacred moments" with God, allowing one to experience "the depths of Jesus Christ." What are the key differences, practically speaking, between these ways of living? Is the second lifestyle realistic or even possible?

The article discusses "mending" (a fly-fishing term) as a means of spiritual development. As Goetz put it, "The trick for the lover of God is to learn how to . . . make small adjustments on a regular basis to avoid the speed and clutter of modern living."

- What are some small adjustments you could make? Discuss specific adjustments you've already made and how they've changed your perspective and enhanced your spiritual life.

Though our culture aims for personal comfort, a vibrant faith matures through suffering.

- Read Romans 5:1–5. How have you seen suffering lead to spiritual growth in someone's life? Or how have you experienced this in your own life?

- Much of our culture (and advertising industry) is built around the human desire to avoid any type of suffering and instead pursue personal comfort. Should Christians try to avoid suffering? Should Christians pursue their own personal comfort? If yes, to what degree? If not, why not?

- Do you think that some amount of pain or suffering is necessary to grow spiritually? Why or why not? And what does this imply for Christians who aren't currently suffering? Should we pursue suffering?

- Goetz wrote: "Sometimes we have to go out of our way to have [suffering] revealed. One way to confront this denial is as old as the Christian faith: voluntarily entering into the suffering of others." When have you been able to do this in the past? What are some ways you can do that now? Share examples and ideas with each other.

■ Going Forward

Break into pairs and talk through the following:

In his article, Goetz reveals, "[D]espite the best the 'burbs have to offer my family—security, options, and efficiency—I find myself restless, always pursuing, always striving, finding less and less fulfillment."

A similar sentiment is echoed throughout Ecclesiastes and is stated poignantly in 2.11. "When I surveyed all my hands had done and what I have toiled to achieve, everything was meaningless, a chasing after the wind (NIV)."

- With a partner, review your past week. Identify together a few of the pursuits, possessions, or uses of time in your week that were ultimately "meaningless," unfulfilling, or spiritually depleting. Next, identify some of the pursuits, possessions, or uses of time in your week that were truly meaningful, fulfilling, and spiritually enriching.

Gather back together as a group to discuss these final questions:

- Which cultural trend we discussed do you feel is most parasitic in your own life, draining your faith of vibrancy and zeal: consumerism and choice, a cluttered lifestyle, or pursuit of comfort? Why?

- Based on your discussion, what's one attitude, luxury, or habit you need to give up in order to draw closer to God?

Pray as a group, asking God to help you support and encourage each other in your common pursuit of an ever-deepening, vibrant faith in Christ.

■ Want to Explore More?

Recommended Resources

David L. Goetz's Web site, including free downloadable discussion guides for small groups (www.deathbysuburb.net)

"Religion in the 'Burbs," interview with R. Stephen Warner by Agnieszka Tennant (www.christianitytoday.com/ct/2003/july/2.30.html)

Crabgrass Frontier: The Suburbanization of the United States, Kenneth T. Jackson (Oxford University Press, USA, 1987; ISBN 0195049837)

Death by Suburb: How to Keep the Suburbs from Killing Your Soul, David L. Goetz (HarperOne, 2007; ISBN 0060859687)

Freedom of Simplicity: Finding Harmony in a Complex World, Richard J. Foster (HarperOne, 2005; ISBN 0060759712)

The Jesus of Suburbia: Have We Tamed the Son of God to Fit Our Lifestyle?, Mike Erre (Thomas Nelson, 2006; ISBN 084990059X)

The Suburban Christian: Finding Spiritual Vitality in the Land of Plenty, Albert Y. Hsu (InterVarsity Press, 2006; ISBN 083083334X)

When did we lose our global vision? And how can we get it back?

SCRIPTURE FOCUS

Matthew 9:35–38

Acts 1:6–12

1 Thessalonians 5:1–3

GLOBALLY MINDED FAITH
IN A GLOBALIZED WORLD

■

The writer of a *New York Times* article on globalization seemed surprised to discover that evangelical churches in the United States are among the country's leading international enterprises. That's no surprise to the members of any mission-minded congregation. What is startling is the question Mark Galli poses in his *Christianity Today* article "Globalists R Us": Are we losing our global vision? Have we lost sight of those things that should motivate our global enterprise? In this study, we'll look at the biblical and historical imperatives that should prevent us from becoming isolationists.

■ Before You Meet

Read "Globalists R Us" by Mark Galli from *Christianity Today* magazine.

GLOBALISTS R US

But there's no guarantee this will always be true.

By Mark Galli

Nicholas Kristoff of *The New York Times* recently said something nice about evangelicals: "A broad new trend . . . is beginning to reshape American foreign policy. America's evangelicals have become the newest internationalists."

He noted facts that are clichés in our world: that the fifteen biggest Christian charities collect more than $3 billion a year; that we were behind both the International Religious Freedom Act of 1998 and the Trafficking Victims Protection Act of 2000; that we are "saving lives in some of the most forgotten parts of the world."

This is old news. As Robert Seiple, president of the Institute of Global Engagement, put it, "Christians began to understand globalization when a Nazareth carpenter said, 'Go ye into all the world.' That was the start of globalization, and there has been no letup in the last two thousand years." Indeed. But unless we read aright the history of missions—Christian internationalism—we run the danger of lulling ourselves into a self-congratulatory stupor.

The Reformers spent little of their intellectual capital thinking about taking the gospel into all the world. That idea did not blossom in Protestantism until the nontheologian William Carey, a self-educated shoemaker, stepped ashore in Calcutta in 1796. But not without a fight— and from fellow Baptists, no less. When Carey first agitated for the idea at a pastors' meeting, one exasperated member burst out, "Young man, sit down, sit down! You are an enthusiast. When God pleases to convert the heathen, he'll do it without consulting you or me."

Not quite. It is very much the likes of you and me whom God enlists, as Carey well knew.

So did the first American evangelical internationalist, Samuel Mills Jr. (1783–1818). When Mills was an undergraduate at Williams College in Massachusetts, he would join other students on Wednesday and Saturday afternoons to pray. In August 1806, Mills and four others were caught in a thunderstorm while returning from their prayer meeting. They waited out the storm under a haystack. That day, they had prayed that students at Williams and elsewhere would become excited about foreign missionary work. While they waited under the haystack, Mills asked if those gathered would commit themselves to missionary service. There must have been some hesitancy, some fear. But Mills would not be deterred, and he uttered a phrase that would become the group's watchword: "We can do this if we will."

At a time when few American Protestants gave much thought to the fate of people in Latin America, Africa, or Asia, Mills's words created, nearly *ex nihilo*, the American Protestant missionary movement, which inspired parachurch groups and denominations to send out thousands of "internationalists" over the next century.

Unfortunately, there has been a reversal in the mainline Protestant denominations, which have drastically slashed their mission budgets during the last fifty years.

Those crazy mainliners. That could never happen to evangelicals, card-carrying internationalists that we are. Then again, during the 19th and 20th centuries, missionary stories were the staple of evangelical reading. I recently asked some evangelical publishers why they didn't carry biographies of the great Protestant missionaries. The answer was worrisome: evangelicals no longer read missionary biographies, or books about things that happened overseas in funny-sounding places. Instead, we spend our money and time buying and reading historical romances, apocalyptic thrillers, and self-help books by the millions.

The great China missionary Hudson Taylor fought not anti-internationalists but his own despair, brought on by the thought of millions upon millions of Chinese dying without having a chance to hear about Jesus. After attending a packed and joyful worship service in his homeland, he wrote that he was "unable to bear the sight of a congregation of a thousand or more Christian people rejoicing in their own security while millions were perishing for lack of knowledge." So he "wandered out on the sands alone, in great spiritual agony."

In our day, when we think of the billions who suffer hunger, slavery, child prostitution, AIDS, or spiritual darkness, too many of us pop into the nearest praise service, packed with Christians rejoicing in their own security, in order to dull our spiritual agony. Hudson Taylor didn't dull the pain, and finally decided, against all odds, to give his life to saving a few. So did thousands of men and women who followed him.

To be sure, evangelical missions is relatively healthy. We are still making a difference in the world. Kristoff's argument is sound. So perhaps it's just a cold, and not the first stages of a cancer, that I detect.

Mark Galli is the Senior Managing Editor of Christianity Today *magazine.*

("Globalists R Us" was first published in *Christianity Today*, September 9, 2002, Vol. 46, No. 10, Page 70.)

For more insightful articles from *Christianity Today* magazine, visit http://www.ctlibrary.com/ and subscribe now.

■ Open Up

Select one of these activities to launch your discussion time.

Option 1

Discuss one of these icebreaker questions:

- If you could travel anywhere in the world, where would you go and why?

- Have you ever gone on a short-term mission trip (or done long-term mission work)? If so, where have you gone? What was it like? If not, is there a place you'd like to go someday on a ministry-oriented trip?

Option 2

To get a taste of how globalized our world is becoming, examine all the possessions you have with you (including clothing you're wearing, your car parked outside, and even miscellaneous trinkets in purses or coat pockets), looking for the phrase "Made in _____" on the label. Create a list as a group of all the countries and regions of the world represented by your manufactured goods.

- Are you surprised by the variety of countries represented on your list? Why or why not?

- In what other ways (besides manufactured goods) does globalization touch your life?

■ The Issue

Globalization. It's a buzz word on the news—a huge cultural trend. Webster's gives *globalization* this nebulous definition: "the act or process of globalizing; being made worldwide in scope or application."

Some people hate globalization with a passion, stridently protesting it as a force behind lost jobs and low wages or bemoaning it as the diluter of distinct local cultures and customs around the world. Others embrace globalization, seeing our growing interconnectedness in the realms of technology and economics as an avenue toward prosperity and greater cultural understanding.

- Do you view the cultural trends toward globalization as a good thing? Why or why not?

The gospel message is "worldwide in scope," and this perspective has historically been central to Christian theology. For most evangelical churches, a short-term mission trip is at least an annual event. The Great Commission passage (Matthew 28:18–20) is almost as well known as John 3:16. Since the missionary journeys of Paul, Christians have perceived themselves as a global people, charged with making disciples in all parts of the world.

- Are you surprised that *The New York Times* is just now discovering the global nature of evangelical Christianity? Why do you think the writer hadn't heard more about evangelicals' relief, development, and mission work?

■ Reflect

Take a moment to read Matthew 9:35–38, Acts 1:6–11 and 1 Thessalonians 5:1–3 on your own. Jot down a few notes and observations about the passages: What words, phrases, or ideas jump out at you? What specific insights do they give you about God's global vision for the church? What questions do these passages bring up?

■ Let's Explore

We are to be globally motivated by Christ's compassion.

- Mark Galli is concerned: just as the world is learning about the international mindset of evangelicals, Galli fears Christians are losing their motivation to go into the entire world. Do you think his concern is well founded? Have you sensed or experienced a waning motivation for missions in the church? Explain.

Read Matthew 9:35–38. Churches often tie this passage to an appeal for workers—children's workers, clean-up crew for the ice cream social, or volunteers for lawn care. Even those who aptly apply the passage to a call for people to share the gospel sometimes skip the motivation behind the call.

Jesus looked on the crowds and he had compassion. His activity was for their well being, both physical and spiritual. He healed them, he preached the good news about God's reign, he met them in the synagogues and on the streets. He was moved to help them because of the concern he felt for them.

If this passage were developed as a flow chart, it might look something like this:

(compassion) (prayer) (God's response to prayer) (harvest brought in)

The Kristoff article in *The New York Times* cites the $3 billion a year given to the fifteen largest Christian charities. Although such support is laudable, American Christians in the past fifty years have given away only slightly more of their money than non-Christians.

The missing element in this equation is compassion. Compassion for those in need will generate a commitment to prayer for workers; God will respond by sending workers.

Our globalization of the gospel is evidence that we take seriously his compassion for us. Our failure to globalize the gospel shows a serious disconnect between his compassion for us and our compassion for others who, like us, need salvation.

- Hudson Taylor couldn't stand to watch the joyous worship of his compatriots when he knew that millions of Chinese were dying without an opportunity for salvation. What do you think Hudson Taylor might say if he stepped into your church's worship service on Sunday morning? How would we respond?

If we were to add another element to the flow chart, we could add to the left of compassion: (presence). Jesus was present with the crowds. When he saw them, he had compassion.

- Think of an experience you've had in which you spent meaningful time with people in need, either in a cross-cultural missions setting or with people in need in your home country. How did spending a few days with those people change how you felt about them?

.

We are to be globally motivated by Christ's command.

- Describe the general attitude toward Christian mission work in our culture. Then think of a non-Christian friend—how do you think he or she views Christian mission work? How does this compare or contrast with the mind-set of Christians in our culture?

- Think about the comments you may have heard when missionaries in dangerous situations have been in the news (such as the Korean missionaries who were recently taken hostage in Afghanistan—and some of them were killed). Do you think Christians today are more skeptical about mission work? Are we more likely to question the motives (or wisdom or sanity) of people who place themselves in danger to share the gospel? Why or why not?

In "Globalists R Us," Galli quotes Robert Seiple, president of the Institute of Global Engagement: "Christians began to understand globalization when a Nazareth carpenter said, 'Go ye into all the world.' That was the start of globalization, and there has been no letup in the last two thousand years."

- Read Acts 1:6–9, one of several passages in which Christ powerfully and succinctly directs his followers to take the gospel message to the ends of the earth. What are some other similar passages that come to mind for you, illustrating God's plan for "globalization"? How do these passages help you see "globalization" in a different light?

- Consider the attitude of those who opposed William Carey's missionary efforts: "When God pleases to convert the heathen, he'll do it without consulting you or me." Where do you see such an attitude exhibited today? How would you refute this perspective?

We are to be globally motivated by Christ's coming.
Read Acts 1:10–11 and 1 Thessalonians 5:1–3.

Jesus promised to return. Until the end of the age and to the ends of the earth, he promised to empower our work through the presence of the Holy Spirit. His followers' part in his second coming is global disciple-making (i.e., in all nations). Our temptation is to stand gazing skyward and longing for his return when there is work to be done. The angels who spoke to the dazed disciples, who literally did the same thing, said in effect, "Snap out of it! Get busy."

In the decades immediately after Christ's ascension, some people were so eager for his return that they could hardly carry on the daily routine of life. Others scoffed and asked why Jesus had not yet returned. In both cases, the work of evangelism suffered. Both the doubters and the cloud watchers had missed the point: the second coming of Christ should motivate our work.

- Which do you think is representative of the Christians in our culture: the scoffers or the cloud-watchers? Which is more representative of your church family? Explain.

- Which category do you usually fall into? Do you focus intently on Christ's return? Or do you more often go about your life without thinking about it?

- Is the church in need of another haystack thunderstorm, another galvanizing event to spur global missions? What do you think it would take to galvanize your home church? How about to galvanize you personally?

■ Going Forward

Break into pairs and discuss these next two questions:

- When have you been inspired by a missionary (or a missionary story, such as those Galli highlights in his article) to personally take a greater part in God's global venture? How does that person's life or experience inspire you? Be specific.

- Consider the three motivating factors you've just discussed: compassion, command, and second coming. Which do you think is most lacking in your own life? How do you feel personally challenged?

Gather back together as a group to discuss this final question:

- Global missions can be accomplished with or without travel. How can your small group support work in distant places via the Internet? What about providing food or medical supplies for those who need it? How can you bring Christ's command to "go" before your congregation more regularly? Discuss areas of need or avenues of ministry you are aware of and talk about how your group might want to get involved.

Spend some time praying together, specifically asking God to renew your global vision. Lift up the various ministry opportunities you discussed and seek God's discernment about the next step your group should take.

Commit to pray daily during the next week about your personal motivations for missions: Christ's compassion, obedience to Christ's commands, and expectation of Christ's coming.

■ Want to Explore More?

Recommended Resources

"Following God Abroad," Nicholas D. Kristof, *The New York Times* (http://query.nytimes.com/gst/fullpage.html?res=9C01E0DF1238F932A15756C0A9649C8B63)

"Are Evangelicals the 'New Internationalists?," Todd Hertz, *Christianity Today* (web only, www.christianitytoday.com/ct/2002/mayweb-only/21.0.html)

"Missions Isn't Safe," a *Christianity Today* editorial (www.christianitytoday.com/ct/2007/november/20.22.html)

Good News about Injustice: A Witness of Courage in a Hurting World, Gary A Haugen (InterVarsity Press, 1999; ISBN 0830822240)

Hudson Taylor's Spiritual Secret, Howard and Geraldine Taylor (Hendrickson Publishers, 2008; ISBN 1598562533)

Operation World, Patrick Johnstone (Gabriel Resources 21st Century Edition, 2000; ISBN 1850783578)

The Legacy of William Carey: A Model for the Transformation of a Culture, Vishal Mangalwadi and Ruth Mangalwadi (Crossway Books, 1999; ISBN 1581341121)

For children

The *Hero Tales* series by Dave and Neta Jackson (Bethany House, 2005)

Bonus Small-Group Builder

From SmallGroups.com

You can find more helpful insights for small group health at
www.smallgroups.com.

MISSIONAL SMALL GROUPS—A WORTHWHILE RISK

By Reid Smith

Outreach has a way of turning groups inside out. Not a bad thing. Struggling groups and small group ministries have found help not by focusing on their own internal issues, but by looking beyond their problems and giving attention to the needs of those outside their immediate relational circles. This article will present how missions benefits small groups and then share ways small groups can reach out together.

First let us define what we mean by mission and missional. *Mission* is the intentional crossing of boundaries from faith to non-faith to proclaim by word and deed the Good News of Jesus Christ. *Missional* is a way of describing the thinking, nature, and behavior of Christian churches, organizations, and believers whose intention, passion, or goals seek to introduce pre-believing people to the person of Jesus Christ.

I have given my life to building the community life of churches through small groups because they are *essential* to empowering God's people in mission. Small groups are not meant to create new comfort zones for people. Rather, they possess the latent potential for embold-ening believers to go *beyond* their comfort zones and to do things they never imagined themselves doing. Every group can find a way to be missional in a manner that is natural for its own unique group dynamic.[i] To not do so is a big miss, a tragedy really.

There is a natural slide toward introversion in small groups, which is a product of a scarcity mentality that many small group leaders have unknowingly adopted. A kind of thinking that is protective, hoarding, ter-ritorial, and inwardly focused. The group-life that results from this mind-set is contrary to the nature and purpose of the body of Christ. Groups that remain self-focused eventually implode because of the vacuous dynamic that has been created from prolonged introversion or their fire fades and momentum coasts to a stop. The same is true of churches.

God wants every believer to share His grace with the world around them (2 Cor. 5:17–20). If this is true, then how could small groups not be utilized, in some way, evangelistically? I encourage all groups to reach out. I do not prescribe *how* groups should reach out. Instead, I present different opportunities that appeal to different kinds of groups depend-ing on their make-up and focus. I might take more of a campaign-style approach and present something church-wide during some seasons.

Mission builds up group participants and benefits small groups. Communicating these insights about small groups and missions to people in groups provides the explanation and encouragement they need to push outward to the edge of their comfort zones. Small group missions—both near and far . . .

- Enables believers to reach out in ways they could not if it were all left up to them alone.

- Enlarges the potential to make connections with people who are al-ready in believer's sphere of influence because it gives them a new social network to work through.

- Expands the number of entry-points into the community-life of their church.

- Provides platforms for invitational evangelism and ready-to-go out-reach teams for missions that help believers enter into new territory and cultures for Christ.

- Bonds a group together in ways that groups with a pure diet of Bible study do not (James 1:22–25).
- Ensures group-life is well-rounded, which helps believers to be well-rounded too.
- Empowers believers in personal evangelism and releases their creativity in outreach.
- Provides a way to take their church's community-life beyond the four walls of the church building so that their surrounding community can see the love of God with skin on it (John 13:35; 1 John 4:12).[ii]
- Allows believers to "go deeper" in their understanding of God's Word more than if they were to give their attention solely to Bible study.[iii]
- Results in stories of life-transformation that inspire others to use their time and resources to reach out and make a difference in the lives of others.
- Strengthens all the other aspects of a group's life together.
- Increases ownership and involvement in the group.
- Brings new believers into God's Kingdom and the group, which the Lord always uses to refresh and enliven a group dynamic.
- Creates ways for group participants to see lives change first-hand, which in turn, inspires them to be more sacrificial and radical in how they follow Christ.

God blesses groups that look for ways to show his lost children the way home—he will make room if we make room (Luke 15:10, 22–24). He inspires new growth in us when we expand the relational circle of our group-life to touch the lives of others. In Luke 17:33, Jesus says, "Whoever tries to keep his life will lose it, and whoever loses his life will preserve it" (NIV). This same economy of the kingdom applies to a small group's community-life and how open it chooses to be to missional thinking and action. Jesus included people who wanted to follow him and a protectiveness over something that is special to us is not reason enough for us to neglect doing the same.

Sometimes people feel like the presence of newcomers will negatively affect the friendship-forming happening in their group. This is a myth. When a group takes a protective (territorial) posture when it comes to its size or acceptance of newcomers, it suffocates itself. A group needs to breathe. New participants feed a group's dynamic like oxygen feeds fire. In other words, new participants bring new life. Consider this: There are a lot more options for dealing with challenges that come with growth than there are in dealing with the problems of decline.

There are many ways small groups can engage in local or cross-cultural missions. The Lord will answer if you ask him how he wants to use you and your group in missions. Start with prayer and think in terms of baby-steps. Your group probably will not start with organizing its own mission trip halfway around the world. However, most people are open and ready to begin praying for the people in their lives who do not yet know Christ. This externally-focused prayer has a way of cultivating missional hearts.

Prayer ignites brainstorming about outreach. This is critical to do in the group and with the group. Small group leaders can bring options, but more importantly, they should involve everyone in the process of determining how the group can expand its circle of influence together. Take time to share the benefits of outreach, answer questions, and give everyone a part to play in organizing for how to engage in missions together.

The Lord will show your group how it can make a difference near and far. You might begin by thinking through what constitutes Jerusalem (local-citywide), Judea (citywide-regional), Samaria (statewide-countrywide), and the ends of the earth (countrywide-worldwide) for your group (Acts 1:8). What does each sphere look like and what opportunities exist within each? Ask the group to come up with examples for each sphere. I have found excellent ideas from www.servantevangelism.com (see also www.kindness.com or www.serve-others.com). For guidance on how a church can engage in cross-cultural/global outreach through its small groups see www.thepeaceplan.com.

There are a variety of ways your group can reach out together:

- Invitational—invite your friends to your group and your church.
- Event based—link your group outreach to your church events and serve together during the weekend services or for special outreach events.

- Community service—go to idealist.org, charityfocus.org, volunteer-solutions.org, or volunteermatch.org then identify needs in your community that touch your group's heart and serve together (e.g. community clean-up day, providing school supplies for underprivileged kids, food delivery, helping the homeless, etc.).

- Web based—social networking sites, e-vites, blogs, interactive online sharing, strategically placed ads and alerts (see more at www.webevangelism.com).

- Sponsorship—support a child (www.compassion.com), a family, or a village (www.harvestofhope.org).

- Focused prayer—adopt a people group in prayer (www.joshuaproject.com or www.adoptapeople.com).

- Mission trips—contact a member of your church's pastoral leadership team and share that your group would like to go on a mission trip together. Learn about what your church is already doing and get a couple of recommendations on organizations that can help with planning it.

Growth is a good thing. People naturally think of it as being a positive. Yet the road we need to travel to get there oftentimes feels very unnatural and even negative. Missions carries this kind of weight in the hearts of many and creates an unpleasant tug-of-war on their insides. However, when we overcome this internal resistance to step outside the safe boundaries of our groups to serve those on the other side of our world (figuratively or literally) we discover new passion and purpose in our lives and our groups.

Recently, our church partnered with a missions organization and we sent two teams of people to Nicaragua's capital city dump. In this dump live thousands of families. Most children have never stepped outside the landfill and end up on drugs or are forced into prostitution so they and their families can survive. In response to this desperate situation, our church partnered with a missions agency and raised money to build a house of hope on the outskirts of the dump where kids could live, learn, laugh, and grow in Christ. The people from our church who went to be used as change agents in the lives of people in the dump were transformed themselves. This story was documented by a local news team who joined our mission teams in Nicaragua (see the story at www. kptv.com/news/14037400/detail.html).

People came back with new eyes and hearts filled with a desire to go back and serve. Their stories continue to touch the hearts of people in our church community, inspiring others to go. People who are not a part of our church and some who are not even Christians have contacted us wanting to join our teams planning to go next year. Church members are being inspired to reach out locally and some of those who went are now adopting kids out of the dump. This shows how missions has a way of releasing kingdom contagions into congregations that compel people to make a difference in the lives of others. For example, one small group is going to Nicaragua together this month. This group had recently birthed a new group out of its existing one so when the other 'half' heard of what they were planning they wanted to go too! The group leaders actually had to create a lottery system to decide who was going to go.

Small group missions is not only about reaching those *outside* of our groups. It is also about reaching those *inside* of our groups so they can discover things within themselves that would have never have come out if they had not ventured beyond their own comfort zones. Your small group participants and the many lives—near and far—that will be touched through their self-giving love makes overstepping the bounds of what feels safe and familiar a worthwhile risk for everyone involved.

i. In *Becoming A Contagious Christian*, Bill Hybels and Mark Mittelberg present six evangelism styles. A questionnaire was designed for individuals, but can be applied to groups as well. Have each person or couple complete it prior to your group's next gathering, and then synthesize everyone's responses together. Another option that might be more fitting for groups that have been together longer or practice open communication is to process through the styles in open dialogue together during group time until everybody arrives at a conclusion as to what style best describes your group's collective evangelism style. Then together you can identify outreaches that harmonize with your group's dominant style.

ii. "Small communities living out their vision in a neighborhood will be powerful community-forming groups in our culture. Churches will effectively evangelize as they form such communities centered on a world-changing vision through Jesus Christ."–Alan J. Roxburgh, *Reaching a New Generation* (1993: InterVarsity, p. 103)

iii. "Ongoing discipleship often involves small groups, one-on-one mentoring, and service with others outside of one's comfort zone. What it does consist of is as important as what it does not consist of—a feed-me-more-meat mentality."–Ed Stetzer & David Putman, *Breaking the Missional Code* (2006: Broadman & Holman, pp. 106–107).

■ Notes

■ Notes

■ Notes

Notes

■ Notes

■ Notes

■ Notes

■ Notes

■ Notes

Notes

■ Notes

Notes